剛軟拳法白龍道

白蓮拳法

This is
BOK LEEN
PAI

KENPO

By:

**Grandmaster
Glenn C. Wilson ()**

Printed in the United States of America

Second Printing ████

ISBN 978-0-9858411-1-9

WDWS Publications

955 W. Lancaster Rd, Suite #1

Orlando, FL 32809

USA

www.pailum.org

Disclaimer

Please note that the author and publisher of this book are NOT RESPONSIBLE in any manner whatsoever for any injury that may result from practicing the techn████████/or following the instruction given within. Since the physical activities described herein may be too strenuous in nature for some readers to engage in safely, it is essential that a physician be consulted prior to training.

Table of Contents

Preface

The journey of a Martial Art can be long and full of obstacles. These obstacles will serve to make the art stronger and deeper in knowledge and substance. If the art does not get stronger it will surely perish as a result of its challenges.

Like a flower it will feed on the nourishments of its surrounding nature and ultimately flourish. It will grow and feed on the sunshine that will help in sustaining its fragile life. It will reach out to absorb nature's life giving element – water. This will nourish and protect the flower as it continues to grow and give beauty to the world around it. If all these factors blend well together the plant will propagate and spread its power to all.

Our story tells the growth and preservation of the White Lotus System of Kenpo Martial Arts. The White Lotus is a most beautiful and strong flower. When so many others die to the cold and challenging elements, the White Lotus sustains.

Kenpo. When I am asked what this art is I answer simply, "It is the bridge between Chinese Kung Fu and Japanese/Okinawan Karate." Kenpo's movements tell the story of the journey of warriors and knowledge itself. This most beautiful and powerful art has met the challenges of time and foes and will continue to flourish for centuries to come.

What is a system or style? It is the many stories of battles and wars that have been won and lost by warriors throughout time. It is the teachings that make new warriors and give us peace and power as one vessel. The teachings that our ancestors have passed down from generation to generation until our teacher stood in front of us and shared their version. It is our honor, loyalty and our courage that is deep in the heart and soul that we call "The Dragon."

My teacher taught me the true meaning of the Dragon and all of its qualities. The teachings of Bok Leen Pai Kenpo is truly the road between China and Japan/Okinawa. It came to us via Hawaii, the modern day homeland of so much Kenpo. This sacred knowledge came to me from a modern day Hawaiian/Chinese warrior named Daniel Kalimaahae Pai. For this great honor and opportunity I will be forever grateful. I will keep the promise to him that I voiced at our last day together. As we celebrated his birthday, I promised and swore that I will forever keep his dreams alive. This he asked of me. That was the last time I saw my teacher alive. As Pai Lum Tao practitioners we will all abide.

Grandmaster – Glenn C. Wilson

Acknowledgements

I find that when authoring any type of writing that will be a part of one's martial arts style and the history of that style it is only accomplished with the great efforts of many people. There is no price that you can put on the passion and hard work that others offer so freely and generously. Such efforts are a testimony to the strength and resolve of our Pai Lum Tao family of martial arts. I thank God and our family every day for being given such a gift.

I would like to acknowledge the following for their tremendous contributions to my second book on the Pai Lum Tao system of martial arts.

- Hilda G. Wilson – tremendous and continuous inspiration

- Bryan Naegele – technical expertise, support and photography

- Rick Armstrong – continuous support

- Rich G. Wilson – continuous support

- Joe McGuire – research

- Conrad Blasko – research

- Don Corless – photography

- All my students who modeled for the photos

- White Dragon Warrior Society members – support

I will treasure the time and training that my younger brother Sigung Jimmy Wilson and I shared. His passing came much too early and his friends and students will miss him greatly. He trained over 30 years in our Pai Lum Tao family; I am proud to be his only teacher.

I would like to give thanks to 'the late' Kenpo pioneer Grandmaster Bill Gregory for his great contribution of Kenpo to American martial arts. I greatly enjoyed our philosophical talks. May his soul rest in peace.

To my Kenpo classmate of the very early 1970s, 'the late' Kenpo devotee & Grandmaster Rich Alford. He was a true leader of martial arts in Florida, a treasure to the art of Kenpo, a world champion in breaking and a good friend. We will miss you.

In memory of my long time friend and training partner, a pioneer of Pai Lum in Florida, Master Fred 'Smitty' Schmidts. You will be greatly missed by many.

In memory of Pai Lum teacher Cosmo Rusch. He was a teacher in Florida who left us much too early. He was a student of Master Smitty.

I would like to give a special thank you to my direct teacher, 'the late' Great Grandmaster Dr. Daniel Kalimaahaae 'Kane' Pai for the many years of guidance, teachings, patience, support and fatherly love that he gave me. Through my young years as an adolescent Sifu to my years as an experienced master he was always there for me and led me with his own unique way of doing things. His way was the old way; it was hard and at times brutal, but always blanketed with love. Dr. Pai will always be remembered as one of the foremost teachers of our times and a martial artist who feared nothing and learned from everything!

Dedication

I would like to dedicate this book to the following:

My family for their never ending support and patience during all my Martial Arts endeavors. As any prosperous Martial Arts teacher will tell you it takes a lot of support from those closest to you to be successful.

My ancestors, a strong blood line beginning with my 'gggggg' grandfather who in the mid 1700s moved from Scotland to the United States and eventually settling in Walker County, Georgia. This very strong lineage of hard working – well educated men set a standard of my present day beliefs and convictions in my fellow man and my God. The blending of blood between the Scottish hunters/farmers and the Native American residents of Georgia created a proud and powerful warrior heart in me that I respectably recognize.

With honor to my Martial Arts family, Gong Yuen Chuan Fa – Pai Pao Lung Gar. I am blessed as a leader/father of my own family of Pai Lum Tao martial arts. I am truly honored to have such wonderful and giving people to train with and share our knowledge together.

I respect my brothers at the Masonic Lodge that I humbly maintain an honorable membership at. They are always giving and share openly their knowledge and fuel my quest for light.

I will always show the greatest admiration and respect to my teacher, (the late) Great Grandmaster – Dr. Daniel Kalimaahaae Pai. It has been years since his passing and journey to our Lord. His teachings and guidance I will forever hold close to my heart. His teachings will endure for centuries to come.

Order of Rank and Virtue

Rank	Virtue
Black IX	Humility
Black VIII	Eminent
Black VII	Superlative
Black VI	Authority
Black V	Nobility
Black IV	Mastery
Black III	Creativity
Black II	Leadership
Black I	Enlightenment
Brown 1	Proficiency
Brown 2	Diligence
Green	Persistence
Blue	Inspiration
Purple	Animation
Orange	Exhilaration
Yellow	Stimulation
White	Birth

Great Grandmaster Dr. Daniel Kalimaahaae Pai
Orlando, FL - 1992

Great Grandmaster
Dr. Daniel Kalimaahaae 'Kane' Pai

Great Grandmaster- Pai Lum Tao Martial Arts
10th Level Pai Te Lung Chuan Kung Fu
Master Level - Bok Leen Pai Kenpo
Master Level – Hawaiian Kempo
5th Level Okinawan Kempo
5th Level Aikido
5th Level Jiu Jitsu
Master Level – Pai Yung Tai Chi
Master Level – Quan Nien Chi Kung

Daniel Kane Pai was born April 4, 1930 in Kameulai Hawaii. He lived the last seventeen years of his life in Florida and passed away in 1993 in the Dominican Republic. Per his request he was laid to rest in his beloved Hawaii. During his sixty-three year journey on earth he built a martial arts legacy throughout North America leaving only five heads of family, a few Sigung's and several Sifu's to carry on the teachings of the 'Way of the White Dragon'. A truly controversial figure, Daniel Kane Pai did it his way, from the tough streets of Hawaii to forming the largest Kung Fu system in North America during the 60's and 70's. There was no doubt of his command of Pai Lum Tao Martial Arts. He taught a rough/tough type of training, for which the Hawaiian Islands are well known. A young Daniel began training with family members in Hawaii in the disciplines of Kung Fu, Kenpo and Judo-Jujitsu. He would master 'the Pai family' martial arts which contained mainly elements of Dragon and Crane. After the mastery of Dragon and Crane the Tiger, Leopard and Snake were introduced to the young practitioner.

His life reflected many changes. He was a teacher of martial arts, a graduate of the Chicago Medical College "Ph.D.", a bodyguard, stunt coordinator, and cowboy at the Parker Ranch, Philosopher, biker and decorated Korean War Veteran. In the seventies, Dr. Pai formed the U.S. White Dragon Martial Arts Society in hopes of standardizing his vast knowledge of martial arts. The students of the sixties and seventies who weathered Pai's rigorous and at times brutal training became known as the "Old School" lineage. Dr. Pai's American team was awarded the Superb Achievement Merit at the Kuoshu event in Taipei in 1976. In 1980 Dr. Pai served as director at the 3rd World Chinese Kuoshu Tournament in Hawaii. During Dr. Pai's visit to Taipei in 1983 he was appointed the United States Vice President of the Worldwide Promotion Association 'Executive Board' of the Kuoshu Federation of the Republic of China. As President of the United States Chinese Kuoshu Federation in 1989 he organized the much-talked about World Chinese Kuoshu tournament in Las Vegas, Nevada.

In 1990 Dr. Pai and disciple Glenn Wilson began work on forming a structured organization to unite the different factions of Pai Lum Tao martial arts, to standardize the curriculum and to legitimize rank. Today this organization is the 'White Dragon Warrior Society'. The Society is 'chaired' by Grand Master Glenn C. Wilson and is dedicated to keeping the dreams of Great Grand Master Daniel Kane Pai alive. Dr. Pai was a true pioneer of Martial Arts in America, a true-life innovator of the modern arts and one of the rare legends in his own time!

Grandmaster Wilson is a senior disciple of the late Great Grandmaster Dr. Daniel Kane Pai and was chosen by Dr. Pai to head up The White Dragon Warrior Society and carry on the Pai Lum Tao torch of learning. Glenn now dedicates his martial arts life to keeping the dreams of Daniel Kane Pai alive and educating the world to this most fascinating style.

Grandmaster Glenn C. Wilson

'Pai Pao Lung Huit'
'Name given by Great Grandmaster Daniel Kalimaahaae Pai'
5 Times World Champion
8 Times U.S. National Champion
Inducted into 6 Hall of Fames
1984 to 1989 Coach on U.S. National Kung Fu Team
CEO - White Dragon Warrior Society
President - Glenn Wilson's Martial Arts Academies International
Head Coach - Wilson's "Pai Lum Tao" Warriors Team USA
Published author
Film Fight Choreographer
Professor: Gong Yuen Chuan Fa Family

Masters Certifications in:
Pai Te Lung Chuan Kung Fu
Bok Leen Pai Kenpo
Pai Yung Tai Chi Chuan
Quan Nien Chi Kung
Shaolin Chuan Fa / Moi Fah Kung Fu

Proud member of:
Gong Yuen Chuan Fa Federation
White Dragon Warrior Society, Inc.
World Kuoshu Federation
United States Chinese Kuoshu Federation
Pai Lum White Dragon / White Lotus Society
World Head of Family Sokeship Council
Martial Arts Collective Society
Pan China Confederation Martial Arts – Beijing, China
International Chinese Kempo Karate Federation

Grandmaster Wilson has had a truly illustrious career. As a competitor in the seventies he was a member of the U.S. Team and won five world titles and eight U.S. National titles. In the eighties he served for four years as a coach on the U.S. Team. Grandmaster Wilson has appeared in virtually every major Martial Arts magazine and has been voted into 6 Martial Arts Hall of Fames. His book "Pai Lum Tao - Way of the White Dragon" was published by Unique Publications and is the first book ever published on the Pai Lum Tao system

As a personal protection specialist he has secured the safety of such celebrities as Michael Jackson, Dolly Parton, Charles Barkley, Larry Bird, Diana Ross, The Beach Boys, The Righteous Brothers, Huey Lewis, Liza Minneli, Barbara Mandrel, Larry King, Don 'The Dragon' Wilson, General Swartzkoff and many more.

He has appeared in and served as fight choreographer for action movies as Don (The Dragon's) movie - "Redemption" in the United States and the movie "Shaolin Kid" in Europe. At this time in his life he keeps busy as a corporate Director of Security / Investigations, Personal Protection Specialist, Crises Intervention Instructor, and President of Glenn Wilson's Martial Arts Academies International which are presently located in North America, Central America, Caribbean, Europe and Africa and is absolutely the largest Pai Lum Martial Arts organization in the world! He also serves as Grandmaster and CEO of the largest Pai Lum Tao organization in the world.

Grandmaster Wilson has been training in the martial arts for more than forty eight years. On Glenn's 10th birthday he began what would become a lifelong devotion to martial arts. He started in Kodokan Judo and then moved on to the Kwon styles of Korea. When he was 16 he witnessed a Kenpo demonstration by Master Thomas Dunn that captivated him more than anything he'd ever experienced in the arts. The smooth, fluid and extremely powerful techniques mystified the young martial artist, who to this day holds a major reverence for its curriculum. Glenn studied the various Kenpo disciplines of Tracy's Kenpo, Shorinji Kempo, Kongo Do Kenpo, Chinese Kenpo and the style that would stay with him for life - Bok Leen Pai Kenpo.

He made the natural transition from his Kenpo roots to the various studies of Chuan Fa. Glenn trained in Gong Yuen Chuan Fa, Lo Han Chuan, Moi Fah Chuan, Five Animal methods, White Crane, and Pai Te Lung Chuan of Pai Lum Tao - a style that captured his imagination and gave new meaning to his martial arts pursuits. The internal influences that would help him center his life and training were practiced in Pai Lum Tao's systems of Pai Yung Tai Chi, Quan Nien Chi Kung and Chin Kon Pai Meditation.

Glenn's life would change for the good in the mid seventies when he went from the private outdoor (very secluded) training of Master Jim Mcintosh to being accepted as a direct disciple of martial arts legend Great Grandmaster Dr. Daniel Kane Pai. Glenn was brought into the Pai Lum Tao System at the rank he held at the time in the Kou Shu of Taiwan - a third higher level black. This was a very rare happening and reserved for only the few warriors with honor, courage and an very high level of martial skill. Then in 1979 Dr. Pai elevated Glenn to Master and named him head of his family of Pai Lum Tao martial arts. That was ordained the 'Gong Yuen Chuan Fa' family of Pai Lum Tao Martial Arts.

Several years before Dr. Pai's passing he and his disciple, Glenn, formed the White Dragon Warrior Society. The formation was designed to preserve the traditions of Pai Lum Tao, share and strengthen the system and legitimize rank among the families. Dr. Pai served as the Chairman of the Board and Co-Founder, while Glenn was Vice Chairman of the Board of the White Dragon Warrior Society, Inc. (after Dr. Pai's passing Glenn became Chairman of the Board), President of Glenn Wilson's Martial Arts Academies International, and Head Coach of the Wilson's Warriors Competition/ Demonstration Team.

Great Grandmaster Pai died in 1993. This left Grandmaster Glenn C. Wilson in charge of the Society they formed - the White Dragon Warrior Society - as well as Senior Master of his "own" Family of Pai Lum Tao.

Glenn Wilson is considered a grandmaster's grandmaster. He is what a Grandmaster should be: He doesn't talk the game, he lives the life - A Pai Lum Tao Way of Life. I am proud to call him my Pai Lum Brother for more than 35 years. He has been a teacher, brother, and a traditional guru in its highest level.

Master Level – Don 'The Dragon' Wilson

Chapter 1

History

White Lotus Style Kenpo History
'Bok Leen Pai Kenpo History'

In early 500 BC Bodhidharma traveled to China to the kingdom of Wei where he met with emperor Wu of the Liang dynasty. For Bodhidharma the meeting was to no purpose; his words to the worldly emperor meant nothing. Disappointed, Bodhidharma left the palace of the emperor and traveled to the Honan province where he traveled to the Shaolin temple to continue teaching.

Bodhidharmas' depression grew once he reached the famed Shaolin temple, for Prajnatra's story was true. The monks were in a ragged condition and were physically and mentally unfit due to the large amounts of time the monks spent in meditation and doing little else. Many of the monks would fall asleep in meditation while others needed assistance in the basic necessities of life - so feeble was their condition.

For an unknown period of time Bodhidharma meditated in a cave at the outer reaches of the temple seeking for a way to renew the spirit of Buddhist teaching. Upon his return Bodhidharma began training the monks in the courtyard. From the physically powerful to the frail he started to enlighten and train with them in the art of Shih Pa Lo Han Sho, or the 18 Hands of Lo Han. These techniques were never originally intended for fighting but were a manner in which the monks could attain clarification while developing their bodies' health.

During the Sui period bandits assaulted the Shaolin monastery; this would become one of many attacks that would occur until the early twentieth century. During this first invasion, the monks attempts at defending their temple were futile, their skills were not accustomed to war techniques and it looked as if the temple would fall. A monk of the temple known only as the "begging monk" attacked several of the outlaws with an array of aggressive hand and foot techniques, killing and injuring some and driving the remaining attackers away. The other monks were so inspired by the display of this single monk that they requested tutelage in this martial style as a means of protection. In scripts this combating art was recorded as Chuan Fa or Fist Method. Chuan Fa translated into Japanese is Kempo, or in English is "Fighting Methods" or "Fighting Laws." This is the basis of most of the Asian Martial Arts in the world today.

Over several generations the warfare arts of the Shaolin temple grew into hundreds of styles in all over the next several centuries. A master of Chuan Fa called Ch'ueh Taun Shang-jen was said to have rediscovered the original Shih Pa Lo Han Sho which had been lost for many years. Ch'ueh integrated his art of Chuan Fa with that of the Lo Han styles increasing his total number of techniques from the original eighteen to a total of seventy-two. Ch'ueh would promote his newfound style by traveling the countryside of China fighting in matches until he encountered a Chuan Fa master named Li in the province of Shensi. Li developed his curriculum of Chuan Fa to that of one-hundred and seventy techniques. These moves were categorized into five unique groups renowned by an assortment of animals. Upon the return to the Shaolin temple of which both Ch'ueh and Li belonged they presented to the other monks the five animal forms - wu xing quan. These forms introduced to the Shaolin temple a new juncture in martial arts development.

Over the next several centuries the history of Chuan Fa and its advent to Kempo is ragged in its tales and difficult to gain accurate descriptions. What is known is that the art of Chuan Fa remained and is still practiced in China, but its teaching also found its way to Japan, the Okinawa Islands as well as the Ryukyu kingdoms. Throughout these islands, the art of Chuan Fa was referred to as Kempo or Law of the fist.

For many centuries it is contemplated that many traveling monks ventured across Japan and Okinawa bringing with them a working knowledge of the art of Kempo. The art would have been taught as an enhancement to the daily spiritual training the monks endured. It is believed that some of the monks would teach at various Buddhist temples bringing forth the word of Buddha, and the power of Kempo to other monks. This would eventually spread to the surrounding villages.

It is generally believed that the Chinese systems of Chuan Fa not only reached the shores of the Ryukyu Islands and became known as Kempo but spread throughout all of Asia to include martial arts influences in Korea, Thailand, Viet Nam, Singapore, Philippines and many other countries.

It is believed that many Japanese and Okinawans made trips to various areas in China for the purpose of learning the mythical art of Chuan Fa. Some people would disappear for many years and then resurface as a master of Kempo and other martial arts. One such traveler was Sakugawa. Master Sakugawa traveled from Shuri, Okinawa to China during the 18th century to learn the secrets of Chuan Fa. He had become a master of respected position in China and throughout his home country of Okinawa. After many years of modification the martial art Sakugawa had learned eventually was renamed to Shuri-te. This art is considered to be the direct ancestor to many forms of today's modern Karate.

It is generally believed that Master Sakugawa, on his return in 1784 to Okinawa, brought with him a Chinese companion named Kushanku. Both men brought with them the art of Chuan Fa which they had studied together in China. They immediately began to demonstrate and teach their arts around their home of Okinawa. It is believed that Kushanku and Shionja had a great influence on the Okinawian Kempo martial arts styles of today.

During the reign of Hideyoshi Toyotomi in Japan there were great plans of conquering mother China. It is commonly believed that many a Samurai Soldier returned from China with extensive knowledge of Chuan Fa and throughout the years modified it to include their own arts of combative arts of Jiu-Jitsu and Aikijutsu. The next great conversion of traditional Chuan Fa from China to Japan would be via a Japanese agent in the mid 1900s by the name of Do Shin So. His art of Shorinji Kempo would grow with great popularity in Japan. Shorinji Kempo would focus on the spiritual aspects as well as the martial art. This is something that Do Shin So believed that the new generations were in great need of. His predictions were right and now his style has become one of the most popular in the world.

Many styles of Kempo and Chuan Fa would find their way to the islands of Hawaii from the late 1800s to the mid 1900s. One of the best known would be the Kosho Ryu Kempo of Masayoshi Mitose. He was born in Hawaii and it is said that he would travel to his family's home area of the Mt. Akenkai's Shaka-In temple near the town of Kinkai, Nagasaki on the island of Kyushu. This is believed to be where the Kosho sect of the Yoshida clan taught.

Hawaii would be commonly known as the location and cradle for the modern development of Kempo, also known today as Kenpo! Many of today's top combative styles and renowned masters would emerge from these Islands as would their training descendants throughout North and Central America. The great state of Hawaii would produce some of the world's foremost pioneers of modern martial arts. A few of those names who are honored with bringing Kempo/Kenpo to the mainland United States are Henry Seishiro Okazaki – Danzan Ryu Jujitsu & Hawaiian Kempo, Richard Takamoto – Hawaiian Kempo, James Masayoshi Mitose – Kosho Ryu Kempo, William Kwai Sun Chow – Kara Ho Kempo, Daniel Kalimaahaae Pai – Bok Leen Pai Kenpo, Edmund Kealoha Parker - American Kenpo, Adriano Directo Emporado – Kajukenbo Kenpo, Ralph Castro – Shaolin Kempo, Al Dacoscos – Won Hop Kuen Do and Paul Yamaguchi – Kempo Jiu Jitsu.

Great Grand Master Daniel Kane Pai's ancestral families of Fong, Pai and Po, would ascertain their knowledge of White Crane and Dragon Kung Fu as well as Judo/Jujitsu and Hawaiian Lua martial arts in the Hawaiian Islands. With a rich bloodline of Chinese and Hawaiian ancestry Daniel would train hard and seek the knowledge of Chinese, Japanese, Okinawan and Hawaiian martial artists to feed his young hunger for the arts. These arts were Kung Fu, Kempo, Jujitsu, Judo and Karate. He quickly became a very skilled martial artist and a feared fighter.

In 1951, Daniel Pai joined the U.S. Army and was stationed on the Mainland. He opened his first school in the back of his Sunset Boulevard home just before leaving to fight in the Korean War. He re-enlisted in 1953, and worked early intelligence in Vietnam in 1954. He retired from active duty in December 1955 and in May 1962 he was given an honorable discharge after completing his military obligation. During his service to his country, Daniel Pai was awarded 4 Bronze Stars, Korean Service Medal, U.N. Service Medal and the National Defense Medal.

Dr. Daniel Pai graduated from the Chicago Medical College, Calcutta India on June 29, 1960, with a degree in Homeopathic Medicine. He would add his homeopathic medicine knowledge into his Bok Leen Pai Kenpo advanced curriculum.

Throughout the mid-sixties and early seventies, he opened numerous schools in the United States, with instructors in Florida, Texas, Louisiana, Pennsylvania, Tennessee, Connecticut, Colorado, California, and Canada. During this time he was operating a school in Daytona Beach and assisting with the operations across the country. This era peaked with fifty plus Pai Lum and Fire

Dragon schools operating in North America. These schools would have a unique blend of Hawaiian Kenpo and Chinese Kung Fu. Over the next two decades some of these students, who trained mostly in Kenpo, stayed close to Great Grandmaster Pai as he trained new students in Kung Fu and Tai Chi disciplines. Great Grandmaster Pai's martial arts system became known as the White Dragon or Pai Lum. Dr. Daniel Kane Pai was one of the early innovators in blending the Kung Fu and Kenpo philosophies together in a successful format for all martial artists.

In 1966 after spending 20 years as a merchant marine, Master Jim McIntosh brought a vast knowledge of the Asian martial arts to the United States through a little known martial art system practiced in the far east known as Gong Yuen Chuan Fa, The Way of the Hard and Soft Fist. Training with Master McIntosh was very rough and physically and mentally demanding. Sifu Glenn Wilson was one of only three Sifus produced by Master McIntosh.

In the mid seventies the Gong Yuen Chaun Fa Federation was established to govern the ranking and curriculum taught. Sifu Glenn Wilson was assigned the duties of director by Master Jim McIntosh and has served faithfully ever since. The teachings of Gong Yuen Chaun Fa's foundation includes four systems: Shorinji Kempo, Lo Han - Buddhist Monk Boxing, Plum Flower system and the Five Animal School. The mix would prove to be an unbeatable combination of fighting, empty hand forms and weaponry.

Since Master McIntosh had retired, Sifu Glenn Wilson was sent to meet the world renowned Kung Fu / Kenpo Grandmaster from Hawaii, Daniel Kane Pai. Their friendship was instantaneous. Grandmaster Pai was very impressed with the young Sifu's level of skills and with the awesome style he taught. Sifu Wilson was blown away as he would perform the ancient Chinese forms for Dr. Pai and he would be asked to stop the form about half way through. Then, Dr. Pai would finish the forms for him. Wilson has proclaimed many times that he was amazed at the vast knowledge of Dr. Pai and that he was so grateful and honored to be accepted as his direct student.

Grandmaster Pai accepted Sifu Glenn C. Wilson as his student. Sifu Glenn maintained the rank he held in Gong Yuen Chuan Fa and with the Kou Shu Organization in Taiwan that was 3rd higher level. The traditional blend of the two great systems - White Dragon & The Way of the Hard and Soft Fist began.

Sifu Glenn began a life long endeavor to study the disciplines of Bok Leen Pai Kenpo, Pai Te Lung Kung Fu and Pai Yung Tai Chi. At the request of his teacher - Grandmaster Daniel Kane Pai, Sifu Glenn would begin to teach the traditional Lohan and Plum Flower forms to some of the other Pai Lum Tao families. Then, in 1979, Sifu Glenn Wilson was elevated to the prestigious rank of Si Gung 'Master' in Bok Leen Pai Kenpo and Pai Te Lung Kung Fu by Grandmaster Pai and the Kou Shu Federation of Taiwan.

Through out the seventies and eighties Sigung Wilson would travel extensively competing in tournaments and competitions and also performing demonstrations. During these years Wilson would win five world titles and eight national titles in open tournament competitions as well as build a record of 13 − 0 in kickboxing. He would utilize his success and reputation as a fierce competitor to promote Bok Leen Pai Kenpo and Pai Te Lung Kung Fu to the world.

In 1990, Great Grandmaster Daniel Kane Pai was in the process of organizing all his Pai Lum Tao schools with several associated systems under an umbrella organization called the World White Dragon Kung Fu Society. Upon the request of Great Grandmaster Pai, Sigung Glenn Wilson was given the honor to oversee the establishing of this organization to protect and preserve the curriculum. This was a project of love for both of them as they worked countless hours together to form this organization and attempt to secure the dreams of Dr. Pai for his life's work. Sigung Wilson was told many times by Dr. Pai that there will be those that will choose to work with you and together for the greater cause of Pai Lum and there will be those that will selfishly keep it to themselves. He would advise Sigung Wilson to watch the gleam of their smile for it may hide that knife at your back. This proved to be very good advice. Dr. Pai directed Sigung Wilson to open the door to all Pai Lum practitioners, but he need do it only once. If they do not show the honor and loyalty to the dreams of 'The Teacher', being Dr. Pai, he need not entertain their efforts any longer.

Great Grandmaster – Dr. Daniel Kane Pai established five families of Pai Lum Tao martial arts. At that time five heads of family were established directly by Dr. Pai to build and maintain their status as legitimate lineage of the teacher. Grandmaster Glenn C. Wilson was named head of family of the Gong Yuen Chuan Fa family of traditional Pai Lum martial arts directly by Great Grandmaster – Dr. Daniel Kane Pai in 1993. Grandmaster Wilson was given all rights to propagate and build his family and to lead and teach Bok Leen Pai Kenpo, Pai Te Lung Kung Fu, Pai Yung Tai Chi, Quan Nien Chi Kung, Chin Kon Pai Meditation and Pai Lum Tao San Shou!

In 1993, while in the Dominican Republic, Great Grandmaster Daniel Kane Pai passed from this life and was laid to rest with full military honors at the Hawaiian National Cemetery. A legacy of knowledge and wisdom was left with many devoted practitioners of Pai Lum Tao across several decades. What they choose to do with it is entirely up to them and their heart.

Under the direction of Si Tai Gung Glenn Wilson, a Board of Directors was appointed during 1994 to protect and preserve the curriculum of the Pai Lum Tao family, as Si Tai Gung Glenn Wilson had promised his teacher – Dr. Daniel Kane Pai. During 1994 and 1995 there were a few individuals who would not conform to the by-laws of the World White Dragon Kung Fu Society resulting in a division of the organization. They would undermine and illegally steal the original name given by Glenn Wilson and approved by Dr. Pai. This is something that Wilson and others would have no part in and they ousted the perpetrators' from the original society. Knowing the nature of some of the practitioners from that past that were ousted from Pai Lum by Dr. Pai many years earlier, Wilson had an alternative name and legal organization in reserve. Dr. Pai was right with his quote. "You can't change the nature of the beast, you can only alter it's behavior for a short period of time."

Keeping his promise to his teacher, Grandmaster Glenn C. Wilson keeps alive the dream of Dr. Pai by promoting the White Dragon Warrior Society, Inc. This organization is devoted to protecting and preserving the dream of Great Grandmaster Daniel Kane Pai. Grandmaster Wilson has served this organization with unselfish devotion to ensure that each school, teacher and student will train hard to understand the origins and curriculum of Pai Lum Tao martial arts. To maintain the highest standards of moral ethics, honor, loyalty, respect, tradition and courage. Wilson leads his martial arts family with the philosophy of keeping your order of life in harmony – God, Family (personal & martial arts), country and work!

White Dragon Warrior Society Research Division

Daniel Kane Pai's KENPO

Few systems can match the diversity and effectiveness of Pai Lum Tao's Way of the White Dragon. This revered system was brought to the public eye in the early 1950s by the legendary great grandmaster Daniel Kane Pai. A time-tested combative art, it proved its worth in the tough back streets of Hawaii. Daniel Kane Pai became legendary for his no-nonsense and highly successful form of fighting which he called, "fighting to survive."

A young Daniel Pai would study the teachings of his family's Dragon and White Crane Chinese chuan fa styles with their Judo/Jujitsu to begin to form the format of early Pai Lum Martial Arts. This base would strengthen and grow as he would in his Martial Arts studies. His training in Hawaiian Lau, Danzan Ryu Jujitsu, Judo, Fut Gar, Hung Gar, Choi Gar, Okinawan Kempo, Hawaiian Kempo, Goju Te Karate and Old Style Tai Chi Chuan would further fortify his art and give birth to today's modern Pai Lum Tao Martial Arts. Within these teachings are three disciplines: Pai Te Lung Chuan Kung Fu; Bok Leen Pai Kenpo; and Pai Yung Tai Chi Chuan.

Recognizing Bok Leen Pai

The characteristics of Bok Leen Pai Kenpo include:

- Strong, yet mobile stances

- Blending of circular and linear strikes

- High level of chi development

- Stiff arm punch with relaxed body

- Sideways "dragon" fighting stance

- Lightning-fast hand combinations and strikes.

- Blocking and striking with the same hand

- Kicks to ribs, done with intricate leg maneuvers

- Rapid success of hand strikes over the entire body

- Stalking in a circle while fighting

- Spirit Shout — "Hey Chi," chanting — "OM," Acknowledgement —"Ush"

Philosophy

Great grandmaster Daniel K. Pai once said, "More than just technique is required to be a master. A master must also be deeply involved in philosophies. A master must seek the truth and allow no boundary to set limits on their search. This is the way of the master, one who is always commencing at the beginning regardless of their years of experience."

Pai Lum Tao's
Modern Lineage

Grandmaster Dr. Seishiro "Henry" Okazaki was a Japanese/ American healer and martial artist. He was born in Kakeda in Fukushima Province, Japan. He emigrated to Hawaii in 1906. He was a very sickly child and through hard training in Kung Fu, Kenpo & Jujitsu, Okazaki recovered completely and vowed to dedicate his life to propagating the Asian martial arts. Grandmaster Okazaki's teachers were Wo Chung – Kung Fu/Chuan Fa and Chinese Kempo, Tanaka Yoshimatsu – Yoshin Ryu, Jujitsu & Judo. These arts as well as the Hawaiian Lua fighting system were the foundation of Grandmaster Okazaki's Danzan Ryu Jujitsu. In addition to the martial disciplines, Okazaki studied health sciences and physical therapy, and ultimately gained a reputation as a healer of the sick and injured. In 1930, Okazaki opened the Nikko Sanatorium of Restoration Massage in Honolulu, which is still in operation today. Many famous personalities of the times came to the Sanatorium to meet, be taught by or be treated by Okazaki. Among the most famous were President Franklin D. Roosevelt, actress Shirley Temple, actor George Burns, and Olympic athlete, actor Johnny Weismuller.

Grandmaster Professor Richard S. Takamoto was the son in law and student of Seishero Okazaki and a well known Hawaiian Kenpo and Hawaiian Lua master teacher in Maui, Hawaii. He operated Kenpo clubs at the Wahiawa YMCA and the Aiea Recreation Center on the Yasuyuki Sakabe Mountain in the late 1940s and the 1950s. Takamoto's reputation as a Kempo/Jujitsu master was widely known and sought after by many martial artists in Hawaii. In 1959 he opened his first school on the mainland USA in Los Angeles, California. Takamoto was one of the earliest and most respected Kenpo teachers in North America.

Grandmaster Dr. Daniel Kalimaahaaee Kane Pai was born in Kameula, Hawaii. Pai is a decedent of Chinese and Hawaiian ancestors. While growing up in Hawaii and having a passion

for the Martial Arts, Pai trained with and was influenced by many teachers. Some of them were Wai Tsu Fu Pai, Herman Kane, Lum Tai Yung, Henry Seishero Okazaki, Richard Takamoto and his family of Pai, Fong and Po. As a young martial artist he became one of the most prominent fighters of the islands, winning trophies and respect for his family name. In the early 1950s Pai brought his unique system of Pai Lum Tao to the mainland USA. Throughout the mid-sixties and early seventies, he opened schools throughout the United States, with instructors in Florida, Texas, Pennsylvania, Tennessee, Connecticut, Colorado, California, Virginia, Kansas and Canada. During this time he was operating a school in Daytona Beach and had many schools located in Florida. This era peaked with fifty plus Pai Lum and Fire Dragon schools operating in North America. Over the next two decades some of these students, who trained mostly in Kenpo, stayed close to Great Grandmaster - Pai as he trained new students in Kung Fu and Tai Chi disciplines. Pai's reputation grew throughout the world as one of the most feared and respected practitioners of traditional martial arts ever. His effectiveness as a fighter and iron palm master became legendary. Yes, Grandmaster Daniel K. Pai did things his way, and became a true martial arts legend in his own time!

Grandmaster Professor Glenn C. Wilson was born in Florida and began training in the martial arts at the age of ten. Wilson has always had a passion for the martial arts and started in the discipline of Judo. He trained for a very short time in the Kwon styles of Korea then as a young teenager he witnessed the beauty of Kenpo and that became his life long love in the martial arts. It was a natural transition to the art of Kung Fu / Chuan Fa. Wilson is recognized as a true master in both of these arts. Wilson has trained in Kongo Do Kempo, Shorinji Kempo, Tracy Kenpo, Shaolin Chuan Fa, Gong Yuen Chuan Fa, Tai Chi/Chi Kung and Pai Lum Tao Martial Arts. Together, Wilson and Pai formed the White Dragon Warrior Society to standardize the curriculum, legitimize the ranking and preserve the traditions of Pai Lum Tao. Wilson was named 'Head of his Family' directly by his teacher, Dr. Daniel Kalimaahaaee Kane Pai and he has served this position faithfully ever since.

Glenn Wilson has been a world champion competitor, coach and trainer to many world champions, voted into six martial arts hall of fames and continues to be an example of professionalism and guidance to martial artists throughout the world. He continues to travel throughout the world teaching seminars and giving lectures on the traditions of one of the most revered and respected martial arts systems today – Pai Lum Tao.

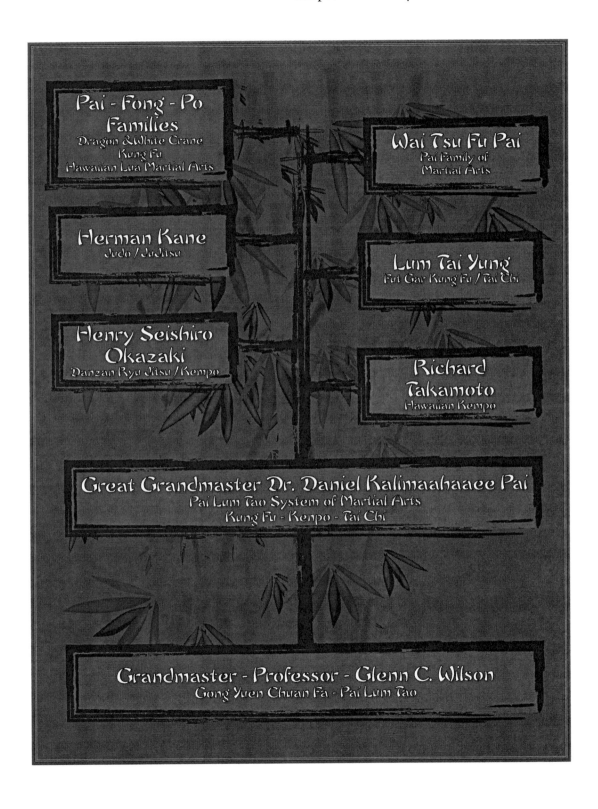

Chapter 2
Philosophy

Philosophy

A proper attitude is crucial for proper progress. A person who thinks he knows everything usually knows nothing or just enough to get themselves hurt. To study Bok Leen Pai Kenpo, a student must practice patience, courage, and above all else humility.

A Student must start slowly, and not expect success overnight. If a student goes too hard, too fast, and does not accept the gradual change of body and mind, injury could result. Many injuries result from a student's display of muscle or impatience.

Many new students want to be like a Master, but few have the perseverance to attain such skill. If a student persists in a daily program, lightly at first, he can attain some success in three years, and possibly become a great fighter in five years.

Surely it is worth the effort, for skill brings health, happiness, and confidence. And remember no student can become an expert without first learning how to behave.

The abilities and disciplines to become a master can take 15 to 20 years or a lifetime. But the journey is truly worth the efforts.

The study of Bok Leen Pai Kenpo has an awakening of the mental, physical and spiritual being. Its teachings focus on a higher level of one's achievement in training. The exercises of Kenpo have been proven through the experiences of practitioners for the last 1500 years. From the demanding physical training to the levels of meditation attained, it truly becomes an avenue of awareness where one may achieve their goals in life. The 'Tao' of Bok Leen Pai Kenpo is wisdom, courage, honor, strength, purity and all knowledge.

Students are trained to know themselves. It is believed that this gives purpose to life and one's direction to follow. Once a student has started their journey, they begin to focus positive energy into their training as well as their daily routines. This will open new doors of enlightenment

What is Bok Leen Pai Kenpo:

When the bitter cold blows in from the North, the snow engulfs Mother Earth sending all into a state of hibernation, the lotus flower blooms, sharing its beauty to all. The endurance, beauty, durability, and strength of the white lotus have made it a symbol of reverence throughout Asia. These are the virtues upon which the Bok Leen Pai system of kenpo was built.   Bok (white), Leen (lotus), and Pai (family) is recognized by its fluidity, power, solid stances, intricate footwork, lightning fast hand work and deep traditional values. With influences of Okinawan as well as Hawaiian combative theories, its ancient roots of knowledge, theories, philosophies and resilience are exclusively Chinese. Yes, it's formation began in the motherland – China.

Students are trained from the ground up - - stance leads to posture and posture leads to technique. Once the foundation is established the intricate formulas for movement are put into action.   The practitioner has now embarked on a fascinating voyage, which will take him through 72 self defense fist sets, 16 forms, a multitude of blocks, punches, kicks, joint locks, pressure point strikes, throws, and weaponry. The average time to achieve a black belt is five years of diligent study. The philosophies of mind, body and spirit encompass the teachings and disciplines of Bok Leen Pai.

The Bok Leen Pai Challenge:

What is the nature of my challenge?

Is it different from my last challenge?

How do I approach my challenge?

How would someone else view my challenge?

How do I feel about this challenge?

What do I know about this challenge?

When do I start doing something to resolve this challenge?

Do I really need to solve this challenge?

Does there really exist a challenge?

Let me now visualize this challenge.

May I seek a wise solution to this disillusion called a challenge?

The major influences in the development of this highly respected system were judo, jiu-jitsu, Hawaiian kenpo and shorinji kempo, as well as kung-fu's southern long hand, lohan and 9 animals. Make no mistake, Bok Leen Pai Kenpo is not a sport, it is an art, the art of the ancient and modern warrior. Honor – Loyalty – Courage coupled within the Mind - Body - Spirit.

This unique and extremely lethal system of Asian Martial Arts was taught 'teacher to student' directly by Dr. Daniel K. Pai to Professor Glenn C. Wilson. Grandmaster Wilson now passes this priceless knowledge on to his honorable and loyal students throughout the world. This is the ancient cycle and preservation of the arts.

What is a Bok Leen Pai Kenpo Sifu?

One who has traveled the most challenging road of all martial artists - the road of 'The Chinese Boxer'! One who has met their challenges with Honor, Loyalty and Courage. There is no shortcut and these three virtues must be in the heart of all would be Sifus. One who readily enjoys passing on the knowledge to those who will travel that road after them. They must teach by example - not just words. They are positive not negative, Proud not ashamed, a builder not a destroyer, one who shares not covets, one who has a deep appreciation and love for the teachings of the White Dragon not one who is scattered with their focus of martial arts. One who truly serves the interest of 'The Family' not one who cares only for themselves and disregards their brothers and sisters. Yes, the title SIFU, will be one of the greatest accomplishments that one can obtain.

The strength of a family is found in its root. The root is the base of the structure that the system is built on. It is important to remember the history and philosophies of the Pai Lum Tao System. A system deep in ancient teachings and molded in modern times. We must always keep in the forefront of our thoughts, "We are a traditional Chinese Martial Art, not a sport!"

Being an art with tradition and time tested challenges, we must do our utmost to not waver from our core! Our core is our center; at our center are the teachings of "Ha Na". This, Dr. Pai taught, was the very essence of a Pai Lum Tao warrior. That is "A Warrior with Compassion". And may an enemy never confuse our compassion for weakness. That becomes their biggest mistake. I say to all, "never confuse my kindness for weakness".

Traditional values are at the beginning of all Gong Yuen Chuan Fa Pai Pao Lung Gar - Pai Lum Tao teachings. Many will enter the door with curiosity and opinions. Few will be able to call the Kwoon's floor home. Even fewer will be graced with the title of "Sifu", a teacher, leader, worker and mentor.

We are all blessed to be a part of a world respected system and to be so close to the source! Great GrandMaster - Dr. Daniel Kane Pai was my only Pai Lum Tao teacher. I spent many years training directly with "THE TEACHER", and was a loyal student until his passing. I still consider him my teacher, advisor, mentor and Pai Lum Tao father.

With such a strong history and family tree it is easy to see why the standards are so high. The future of the system and family require a Sifu to foster the strongest leadership qualities. They must possess and teach the younger students such qualities as: Loyalty, Honor, Courage, Empathy, emotional and physical stamina, self confidence, Responsibility, Accountability and Tenacity.

Grandmaster Glenn C. Wilson

A Good Sifu:

Owns their actions, not their words

Must attach value to high standards

Must strive for continual improvement

Will make great personal sacrifices for the good of their students

Cannot favor themselves over their students

Will hold a profound conviction of their teachings and system

Is responsible for establishing the atmosphere in which they lead

Must teach, establish and follow the order in which a student may be judged, rewarded, or challenged.

This vision we all share.

The Harmony Of Nature

In meeting which prevails, ice or fire

You would probably say fire and you would be correct

However in dying does not the ice turn to water

Which will kill the fire

This is the harmony of nature

Each element in turn of importance conquers the other

That prevails which recognizes the power of the other

Conquer your spirit, discipline your mind

Train the muscles and limbs to move gracefully

Correct your attitude and be aware of the power of Kung Fu

If you do as I say, you will also prevail

I Be

I am because of the nights and days I have seen

I believe I am a man for the things I have done

But all it is, is just feelings of sensations that are created by my mind

Those that I touch know me as I am

These simple arts that are known as Kung Fu

Are the feelings I have of the things I now love

These high sensations and thrills of my spine

Are not love but a practitioners body that cares for his art

If it sounds as if I am a dreamer

Then let me dream as I practice this Martial Art that is called Kung Fu

These strange feelings I have of knowing the world called devotion

A Good Student

A good walker leaves no tracks

A good speaker makes no slips

A good listener forgets nothing

A good strike never misses its mark

A good body never tires of technique

A good technique never requires explanation

A good student seeks none

The Ancient Masters

The Ancient Master were subtle, mysterious,

silent, profound and responsive

Watchful, like men crossing a winter stream

Alert, like men in the jungle

Courteous, like visiting guests

Yielding, like melting ice

Simple, like uncarved wood

Hollow, like caves

The Ancient Masters were aware that the flesh

dies away and is soon forgotten

The spirit remains forever

A Meditation of Rank

No person, regardless of rank, can stop practicing or learning. To stop learning would mean to stop trying. Degrees of rank are merely points on the circle of learning. All points begin an equal distance from the center or Tao. Never let rank or the lack of it cloud the truth.

For instance: To establish rank we must establish learning; To establish learning we must also establish what knowledge is; To establish knowledge we must first find experience; To find experience we must find pride.

To actually break rank down we must first seek a man whose knowledge is greater than ours. Rank is a position of knowledge or the lack of it. Rank has nothing to do with the belt you wear except to distinguish the learning ability and knowledge of each person.

The circle of learning is the beginning of the way. What way you want to go, what you want to do with your life. From the moment you are born you begin the endless circle of learning; it is the same in the way of the White Dragon "Pai Lum Tao"

For example: if you go to college, you will be asked what you plan to be, what goal you are setting for yourself. If you set your goal to be a doctor, then you will take courses that will help you reach the goal. It is the same with karate, Kung Fu, or any of the ancient teachings. Without the foundation and structure of fundamental knowledge you cannot achieve the rank of black belt. The rank of black belt is one of higher learning and knowledge than that of the beginner. We should appreciate the knowledge and disregard the degree.

When you have established the way of understanding (which is the Tao), then you will not cloud the truth by the mere color of a man's belt. It is not the belt that matters at all – it is the knowledge that each man retains as he passes each point on the circle of learning.

You must be careful not to judge a man by the color of his skin or the color of his belt. Judge not what you do not know and no one will judge you.

The way of rank is a tool we can use to distinguish the degree and depth of learning and achievement. Don't classify it as a "position." It is nice to be proud of the knowledge you have, if it is growing knowledge that can be passed on to others.

Do not assume that all knowledge is the same. It is wrong to think that everyone's knowledge is equal.

We are brothers and sisters in flesh and blood because we are all human, and because of this we are all equal. This is true, but even though we are all of flesh and blood and are all equal in that respect – we are not all equal in our knowledge or our capacity to learn.

Each of us knows there is someone who can do some thing better than we can, but we also know there are many things we can do better than someone else.

Another example: No matter where we are on the financial ladder of life, we are all still equal. It is foolish to think you are better than someone else because you make more money than they. In the same sense it is wrong for you to think you are better than anyone else just because you have a higher degree belt than they do. Your knowledge may not be as superior to theirs as you think. Take pride in your knowledge, don't take advantage of it.

We must learn to recognize knowledge so we may achieve unity and continue the circle of learning. If we take away the equality of men there is no circle, if we take away the right of each man to learn and to pass on what he has learned to another, then there is no beginning and no knowledge – just the end.

So, rank's purpose is to show us the knowledge of each individual as he achieves each point along the circle of learning. Therefore, our respect for knowledge is the way, that is the Tao.

Don't get a misconception about rank. Tradition does not relate us to one. Equal to one. Each individual should have respect for what we call this something in the Chinese book for the ancient one, the whole seeing one. But he is nothing but flesh and blood. For the ancient one is always looking for the Higher one with the greatest powers of all – God. One reason monks died with smiles on their faces is because they knew at last they were going to meet God. To feel a vibration about dying is no longer a burden. Why is it that people have a burden about leaving this world? You don't want to begin to live, don't begin to live, until you die. Follow? Don't begin to exist until you die. How to prepare to die? See the oriental people that smile? They have fulfilled what they came here to do. Now they are going where they are much happier. That should not be treated as something hard and drastic. It is the most perfect release of responsibility you could have. White Dragon people accept it is when you are afraid that it becomes a burden. You should have words that help, not preach religion and a sense of direction. You cannot go through this world carrying that burden alone. You must seek someone to share it with you. You cannot do it alone. It is impossible to travel this world alone. Whatever you feel you must know, seek and ask questions.

Understand - there are some things worse that dying. To accept torment, you accept the responsibility of being constantly ignored. Live comfortable. Have something worth living for. The more comfortable you get the angrier you get.

Dr. Daniel K. Pai

The Tao

The Tao cannot be defined by words

Any words used are one-sided and therefore misleading

Tao is merely a word given to the nameless source of the Universe

The Universe is the mother of all things, visible and invisible

When you have ceased judging things by yourself

You may see the unseen

Judging things by their relationship to you, you see the visible

But visible and invisible are only words that are different by definition

In essence they are the same

This mystery is a shadow within absolute darkness

Here is the doorway to truth

All things are one

The Tao smooths the rough surface of life, like gentle rain

The perfect way 'Tao' is without difficulty,

Save that which avoids picking and choosing

If you quest for the plain truth

Be not concerned with right or wrong

The conflict is a sickness of the mind

Thoughts

The heart of a fool is in his mouth, but the mouth of the wise man is in his heart.

After all this is over, all that will really have mattered is how we treated each other.

They may forget what you said, but they will never forget how you made them feel.

Better bend than break.

There is never time to do it right, but there is always time to do it over.

Facts do not cease to exist because they are ignored.

Fail to plan, plan to fail.

I have never started a fight and I have never fought the same man twice.

Be of sound mind, good judgment and superior

moral character then you may adhere to your own free will

As a teacher I shall progress, therefore

I will never condemn, ridicule, embarrass or shame my students

Hold sacred the right to protect ones self,

family, friends or that of the subjugated and disadvantaged.

A White Dragon Warrior shall never do anything that would be inconsistent with their moral, social or religious beliefs

Life and Death

A man is born gentle and weak

At his death he is stiff and hard

Green plants are tender and filled with sap

At their death they are withered and dry

Therefore the stiff and unbending is the disciple of death

The gentle and yielding, the disciple of life

Thus an army without flexibility never wins a battle

A tree that does not bend with wind will break

Power

In a pursuit of true power

a student must reach deep within the mind

No longer with human weakness

You identify with the power of the Tiger

Through the flow of Chi life force

To accomplish this, you must meditate

Strengthen the muscles and bones and read the Tao

To be at one with all nature

You must at one with yourself

True power is a combining of psychic and physical principles

that are attained through hard training

Miao Xing's Teachings

One must not use his power for deception of people,

One must not rise over other people,

One must not use this art for suppression of people,

If there are achievements there should be flaws,

It is necessary to know about flaws to attain higher achievements

It is necessary to breed the true greatness of spirit

White Dragon's Flame

Look into the flame of the candle

Concentrate, search for its center

Now calm your spirit, what do you see

Peace or discontent, I see both Grandmaster

What you see my son is your own heart

Train yourself harder like an incessant storm

You tell your American students to seek peace always

But you must first find peace yourself

If you do as I say, you will have true power

And the flame will reflect only content

Dragon Code

English

I am what I am because I choose to be. I am a Dragon by choice, and subject to it's laws. My brothers and sisters are my heart and my mind. Even though we may disagree with each other, we still strive to be one. Forgetting all categories and letting energy which wishes to exist, exist. But as a Dragon, I must go forth to seek the Tao and the void, understanding myself, and finding peace within.

Das Dragon Gesetz

Deustch

Ich bin was Ich bin, weil Ich es so wollte. Ich bin ein Dragon bei Wunsch und ein Subject zu seinem Gesetz. Meine Brüder und Schwestern sind mein Herz und meine Gedanken. Auch wenn wir nicht immer einer Meinung sind, bemühen wir uns doch einig zu sein. Wir vergessen alle Categorieren und lassen die erwünschten Energien existieren. Als ein Dragon muß ich vorwärts gehen um den Tao zu suchen, mich selbst zu verstehen,und Frieden in mir selbst zu finden.

Codigo de Cos Dragones

Español

Yo soy lo que soy, porque yo lo elegi, yo soy un dragon por la opción y conforme a sus leyes. Mis hermanos y hermanas son mi corazón y mi mente. Aun puede haber discrepancia entre uno y otro, todavía nos esforzamos en ser uno. Olvidándose de todas las categorias y dejando la energía que desea existir, que exista. Pero como un dragón yo debo ir hacia adelante y buscar el tao y el vacío, entendiendome a mi mismo y encontrando paz interna.

白龍道

龍的格言

我就是我，因這是我的選擇，我選擇似龍，就要遵守這準則，我的弟兄姊妹就是我的心和智。雖然我們間中不妥協，但我們仍然團結一致。忘記你有分類，而由原動力去生存，去發揚光大。但由於我是龍，我務必要去尋找那道與道之間的真締，明白自我又尋找內裡太平。

Dragon Code

The Dragon Code – A Student's View

I Am What I Am Because I Choose To Be

It is my choice to decide the direction of my life. To hold any other person or thing responsible for who I am is to cloud the truth. Knowing this to be true, I have the ability to change my life

I Am A Dragon By Choice And Subject To It's Law

I have chosen the way of the Dragon (Kung Fu) as my path, and willingly accept the rules, which are the guidelines of my style. Furthermore, I must respect and abide by the greater cosmic laws, which govern this path.

My Brothers And Sisters Are My Heart And my Mind. Even Though We May Disagree With Each Other, We Strive To Be One.

My brothers and sisters are a reflection of myself, and I of them. We have one purpose: to develop our bodies, minds, and spirits through the practice of our art. Beneath the superficial ego and personality differences, we all arise from the same source. Recognizing this, we strive to put away petty self-interest and work together to reach our common goal.

Forgetting All Categories, And Letting Energy Which Wishes To Exist, Exist

Putting aside all thoughts of rank or self-importance, we must learn to flow with the Energy of our path. Though categories are easy to voice, they are simply a convenient way of classifying things. They are not the reality of things. Understanding this, we know that all things arise from the same energy and we must allow this its existence and not judge the world by our own concept of this.

But As A Dragon I Must Go Forth To Seek The Tao And The Void, Understanding Myself And Finding Peace Within.

I know as a Pai Lum Tao practitioner I will seek further knowledge and always be guided to the light. I know the difference between being half empty or half full. I know that before I can find favor and understanding in others, I must know who I am.

The Dragon Warrior's Code

The warrior is a man who dedicates his life to the cause which makes him what he is. What governs the Warrior is the foresight that he has, to see beyond the present and into the future, beyond the capabilities of those who follow him. The Warrior is dedicated to defend the honor, the creed, the pride, and the self-respect for what he wishes to be called:

"Dragon – Dragon – Dragon"

Chapter 3
Formulas

Bok Leen Pai Kenpo's Formulas

There are many different Formulas found within the core of the Pai Lum Tao Martial Arts System. They are short sayings that have been time tested by the masters of these incredible martial arts and have been passed down as a guideline for practice. They will educate and point the way to illumination whether it be physical, mental or spiritual. Here are but a few that the leaders of Pai Lum Tao gladly share with the Martial Arts world while there are others that will remain a secret only to the few who learned them directly from THE TEACHER – Dr. Daniel Kane Pai.

- The weapon is an extension of the body

- Move in the nei and strike in the wei

- There is a difference between the exercise and the application

- The difference between a block and a strike is the intent

- A student is a product of the teacher

- Stance, Posture Technique

- The White Dragon can change shape and form at will

- Square up your life or travel a crooked path

- Fell ones opponent through manipulation

- Seek to know your energy and elevate to a higher level of consciousness

- Never sacrifice technique for speed

- Degrees are merely points on the circle

- Pursue the logical path of proficiency

- Never ridicule, embarrass, condemn or shame a fellow Dragon

- The eyes are the windows of the mind

- The ears are the eyes of darkness

- Penetration is our depth of focus

- Focus is our concentration of mind, strength, method and chi

- Body momentum derives its power from horizontal movement

- Penetration insures increased power

- Cover insures against vulnerability

- The three depths are short, medium and long

- Transition is a reinforced move that can be defensive or offensive

- Torque is relayed body action

- Power is proportionate to the physical strength, force and energy exerted

- Timing is a rhythmic marriage of our economy of motion

- Avoid wasteful thoughts, motion, angles, power and energy

- Environment encompasses those elements that are around you, on you, or in you; prior, during and after an encounter

- To beat action, meet it

- Preserve our sacred effects, God, family, country and society

- Examine, explore, expand and expound on life's theories

- The heart of a fool is in his mouth, but the mouth of the wise man is in his heart.

- After all this is over, all that will really have mattered is how we treated each other.

- They may forget what you said, but they will never forget how you made them feel.

- Better bend than break.

- There is never time to do it right, but there is always time to do it over.

- Facts do not cease to exist because they are ignored.

- Fail to plan, plan to fail.

- Emotional tensions are caused by our chaotic manner of living.

- Shaolin, Sil lum or Shrin ji is the root of our martial and theological teachings.

- The tests of Pai Lum Tao consist of physical, mental and oral examinations of our systems teachings.

- It is said that it would take three lifetimes to master Pai Lum Tao's intricate hand movements.

- The eyes are our receivers of action and movement, they trigger our reaction.

- In every phase of life, if enough time and thought were given to every effort, greater knowledge would be the end result.

The Five Elements - Wu Hing

Chinese philosophy divides the world into five elements: Wood, Fire, Earth, Metal and Water. These elements are symbolic and represent five forces in nature. The constant interplay between these five forces constitutes the structure and the make-up of creation. The first element is Wood. It represents the life force or spirit, which is responsible for the growth of living organisms in nature (such as trees). This formless life force is usually concealed from our sight by its form, which is Wood, its material structure. Wood burns and gives rise to Fire. From Fire come ashes - Earth. Earth gives rise to Metal (called "Air" in Western occult philosophy). From the Earth with its Metals, Water springs up. Water gives rise to plants and Wood is created. Therefore, Water gives rise to Wood, and the cycle is constantly replenishing and renewing itself. This is creative interplay of the five elements (Seng cycle). The five elements interplay destructively, meaning they breakdown creation. Disintegration is necessary before regeneration can occur. Therefore, disintegration and generation are but two aspects of the same process (Yin and Yang). The destructive interplay (Ko cycle) is as follows:

Wood destroys Earth - plants break up rocks

and soil, ancient wooden plows tilled the soil.

Earth destroys Water - Earth absorbs Water,

Earth impedes the natural flow of Water.

Water destroys Fire - Water extinguishes Fire.

Fire destroys Metal - Fire melts Metal.

Metal destroys Wood - Metal cuts Wood.

What Is Meditation?

In Europe and the Western Hemisphere, the word "meditation" comes from Latin and means "thinking." "To meditate" is "to think." Thinking is a natural, normal process in which most individuals engage every waking moment as well as throughout much of their sleep. Most people would be surprised to find that they already practice some degree of meditation!

The difference between the practitioners of any particular type of meditation and non-practitioners is that, during at least some part of the day or week, the meditator takes time out to think about one particular thing. The practitioner chooses the object of their thoughts, focusing on a particular thought, subject, emotion, activity, or experience. Even the meditator's own consciousness may become the focus of their practice.

The amount of time meditating or the frequency of meditation is not what makes the practitioner. Practitioners of meditation differ in regards to their interests and conditions. These differences are reflected in their choice of schools of meditation and philosophy. The determining factor is simply that the practitioner has made the effort to focus, concentrate, and direct his or her thoughts and thinking.

The thoughts of the non-practitioner may jump from one thought to the next. The non-practitioner may believe that they are doing the thinking, but their thoughts are reactions, products of both internal and external conditions.

When the mind and/or body are restless or agitated, what feels like a poor or light meditation will help the mind and body to rest, and is especially strengthening in what might future difficult times. Do not compare meditation sessions by how you feel afterwards. It takes more effort to meditate during bad times even thought the experience of the "meditative state" may seem to be absent. In all forms of meditation the mind drifts off. When we catch ourselves being distracted, we return our awareness to whatever was the focal point of meditation. We are practicing the return to point or center of meditation. Weathering the bad days, with each return we are strengthening the mental concentration. Many times the bad days give us a better practice, even though we may not feel satisfied with our session.

The commonalities of the various types of meditation are much greater than are their differences. Many times as humans we tend to dwell on differences, even though one purpose of meditation is to transcend differences.

Several systems for "classifying" types of meditation are used. While these systems may seem to help in the beginning, they eventually become a boundary that the one must overcome. Three methods of classification are: organization, way and path.

Methods of meditation may be either structured or unstructured. In a structured meditation, the activities performed are carefully and precisely defined. The practitioner is instructed in regards to the correct focus of meditation, the nature of any incorrect focuses of meditation, and the processes used in the meditation.

Forms of meditation that have continued some connection with their founding traditions require that the practitioner prepare themselves in some specific manner before meditating. Many times, preparation includes some form of mental-spiritual and/or physical cleansing in order to purify the body, mind, and soul. Proper preparation may have several purposes. It may be believed that the practitioner needs to be purified, cleansed or made worthy. It may be viewed that preparation shows that the practitioner is making personal efforts in order to be worthy of the meditation experience. Preparation may to be seen as helping to clear away false or preconceived notions so that the practitioner does not "contaminate" their experience.

Psychologically, preparation may help the practitioner start a process of focusing more on the meditation and less on any worldly or distracting concerns. This may be especially true if the practitioner meditates with some frequency and always performs the same rites or activities beforehand. These activities serve as stimuli to slow down the body and mind so that one may enter a meditative state. To some extent, the preparation may become the beginning of the meditation itself.

Before a meditation session, address the following questions:

Have you selected practice times during which you are relatively unlikely to be distracted?

Have you finished some other duty that would distract you if it were not finished?

Do you have a special quiet place in which to practice?

Try to make sure that you won't be interrupted.

Do not have a drink containing caffeine (coffee, tea, cola, and some non-cola soft drinks) for at least 2 hours before practicing. Caffeine can make it more difficult to relax and focus your attention on what you are doing.

You should not eat any food for at least an hour before practicing.

When you are finished, come out of your relaxed state very slowly and gently. Take about 60 seconds to easily open your eyes all the way. Then stretch and take a deep breath.

Now go forth with your meditation and conquer your challenges with the power of love & light.

Chapter 4
Fighting Techniques and Theories

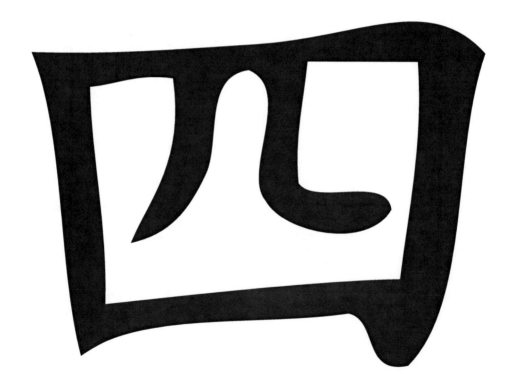

Bok Leen Pai Fighting

Many Fighting styles and theories have vanished and flourished throughout the diverse and extensive martial arts record of China.

A legacy of fighting styles and systems have been compiled by generations of skilled warriors who drew from personal combat experiences. The warrior, who believed that his technique or style would be superior on the battlefield, engaged the formulas and theories generated by such activity in combat. The warrior would train diligently and thoroughly to master each and every technique. They could not afford failure; for the price for failure was more often than not death. Their training would shape the basis for a unique fighting style, the worth of which would in due course be proven on the field of combat.

One of the results of this constant and diverse development is the Pai Lum Tao system of Martial Arts. The short range combat system is known as Bok Leen Pai Kenpo. Within its arsenal one will find a highly effective series of cutting punches and kicks coupled with it's traditional animal movements as well as it's powerful San Shou training. This has proved to be a combination that is second to none in the ever challenging world of pugilism.

One of the most lethal aspects of Pai Lum Tao training is the Ghost strikes series. These awesome techniques are generally not offered to the novice student. Time on the floor and proven dedication are two of the essential ingredients for one to be taught this guarded arsenal. The Ghost strike series is truly revered as one of Pai Lum Tao's and Great Grandmaster – Dr. Daniel Kane Pai's greatest treasures!

One starts off by understanding the philosophy used to strike to a target, using vertical, horizontal and circular motions. Distinguishing the cutting series from other theories and formulas is its unique composition of linear and circular striking, which are utilized within the implementation of one distinct and shocking move. If done correctly the impact and penetration can be lethal to the receiver. Although the technique possesses power and explosiveness, it is the penetration of the Pai Lum Tao punch or kick that showcases its significance. The technique is executed into the target, but does not stop there; instead, it cuts through the target. Such shocking penetration makes these techniques among the most effective and deadly in any martial arts repertoire.

The fighting series developed through the evolution and expansion of various fighting styles. Borrowing from strengths of both Northern and Southern kung fu, this series emerged as a potent combination of motion-generated power and explosive short-range combat. The Northern influence lends its mobility in stances, flexible movement and long-range striking. The Southern style enveloped the theories of short-range explosiveness into the target area, powerful stationary stances with an emphasis on power. The Northern developed sinew strength and power through movement. The Southern style practiced powerful explosion into the target. From a blending of motion and explosion, the cutting punch emulated admirable qualities of both styles.

White Dragon punches make use of both Gong (hard) and Yuen (soft) hand techniques. The basic routines that are practiced by the beginner are – The figure eight pattern, circular and the sphere patterns. The progression of strikes found in the cutting series of Pai Lum Tao are executed quickly; several techniques a second are delivered to overwhelm an opponent. The movements are smooth, fluid and powerful.

The effectiveness of Pai Lum Tao's fighting concepts finds its basis in strong, solid stance work: from the toe, the energy moves into the calf, travels up the thigh, surges through the waist, shoots up the back, travels into the shoulder, elbow and wrist, and culminates in the hand technique being performed. The fighting techniques strike and penetrate into and through the intended target.

As the fighting series is executed, the body should be relaxed, yet firm: tight muscles or joints should be avoided, as this restricts energy flow, and interferes with sinew and/or muscle movement vital to the proper execution of the technique. Relaxation is necessary to allow the body to perform the whipping motion required to guide the path of the punch or kick.

The white dragon way of punching utilizes linear and circular motions united into one unremitting, fluid movement. Different parts of the hand may be used to transform this energy during one's striking. There are closed fists, open hand and different animal claws which will be utilized to defend against an adversary. One's punches will travel directly into and then tear through the target. Basically, the punch penetrates a few inches into the target with a linear motion and then cuts through with a continued circular motion.

The system of Pai Lum Tao techniques also includes many powerful and lethal kicks. These kicks can be further positioned into a subcategory of standing, jumping and lying kicks. The theory of relaxed, fluid motion focused on penetration into a particular targeted area also applies to the kicks.

Some of these kicking techniques may be targeted to the high zone area, but most of the White Dragon kicks will be executed to the mid and low areas. Keeping in mind that the Pai Lum Tao system of Martial Arts is a highly effective and time proven form of self defense.

In Pai Lum Tao Martial Arts, the practitioner will not need to adjust the hand or body in reaction to the target moving. There is a designated target, but should that target move, the technique is designed to shatter and destroy whatever lies in it's path.

Serious conditioning of the body and training of the mind is required before these techniques can be properly mastered. Solid stance work, aligned body posture and Quan Nien Chi Kung breathing methods must be firmly recognized before beginning the demanding repertoire of instruction.

The legacy of the awesome Pai Lum Tao system of Martial Arts lives on in the philosophies, formulas, concepts, theories and techniques practiced by all those that are fortunate to keep the dream alive. This is a most unique and enlightening art. The secrets and teachings of Dr. Daniel Kane Pai have: in the past - they taught us, In the present – they sustain us and in the future they will deliver us. We all have benefited from his guidance and knowledge. Our challenge is to preserve and keep the art pure!

Formulas and Fighting Theories of Great Grandmaster Dr. Daniel Kalimaahaae Pai

Positioning

Placement of the body has caused many uncertainties among martial artists. The unusual placement of the hands and legs has prompted some to believe that magical power can be summoned by holding one's body in strange postures. The truth is that to assume a stance because of its visual effect accomplishes little if anything.

The martial artist must be free to move as his instincts and reflexes demand. When confronted with a challenge, no experienced fighter would spread his legs as wide as possible and squat.

Stances are formed in order to concentrate maximum power for a split second only. Stances aid in focus, but focus is only momentary. To hold focus, one becomes like a stone figure.

Most boxers fight with one or the other side forward. Few if any boxers have been successful in switch hitting. Kung Fu / Kenpo men, however, have enjoyed some success in switch hitting. The point is disputed as to which is a better method.

A 50-50 weight balance is generally best with the ability to switch to 60-40 or 40-60 in the charging horse.

Six Primary Techniques

These are the most successful of all techniques used and are responsible for the majority of victories in kung fu / kenpo contests. The point to remember about each is that the wrist pulls the arm and the ankle pulls the leg. The fist or foot must be brought into play as soon as humanly possible. The techniques are the following:

Reverse Punch (vertical and inverted)

Lunge Punch

Ridge Hand

Wheel Kick

Side Kick

Much work is required on each of these in order to succeed with them.

Leading Side vs. Rear Side

The leading side yields an open position, e.g. the charging horse. Rear side yields a closed position, e.g. soft bow. The open is good for attack with both hands and both feet, but provides a greater target for counter attack. The closed stance allows limited attack, but guards the center line. On rear lead, you can turn your back and let your opponent charge you. You place your lead leg between his legs and throw with O or Ko Uchi Gari. Also Uchi Mata is possible.

Economy of Motion

You must always strive to do the least both in energy and movement, but yet accomplish the most. To block and counterattack with the same action is better than blocking, then counterattacking. The study of martial arts is a lifelong process of economy of motion or using the body to its best advantage.

Hyper-Extension

Contributes power and reach to the technique. On each technique you must strive for maximum reach and power. This is only found through continued practice. For example, in a reverse punch, extend the right first and twist the right hops as far forward as possible. Extend the right shoulder (reach is equal to the forefist).

Relaxation vs. Tension

Tension should occur only for a short time during the fight. Tension causes a drain on the fighter. The soft style plays down tension and opts for relaxation while fighting. Tension should only be used when one focuses a technique. The instructor should check the student and if he remains rigid while performing, he is executing kung fu / kenpo improperly.

One method of practicing relaxation is to tell the body that you are only going to move the hand, e.g. in a back knuckle you keep the body relaxed and concentrate only on moving the hand. This greatly increases the speed of the technique.

Hold no stance or any body position that requires tension. Remember, relaxation is the natural disposition of the body.

Independent Movement

The arms and legs are fast and deceptive, but not as powerful as the hips which are slow. The objective of the techniques is to make contact with the target. Deception and explosiveness are the two key elements for a successful technique.

The independent movement of the arms and legs separate from the movement of the body contribute to the explosiveness of the technique. An arm can be extended before the opponent can react. With arm dragging the body rather than the body pushing the arm, explosiveness and deception are complimented.

Mobility vs. Immobility

Footwork and movement is important for deceptiveness. 90% of footwork is ad lib. You can counter shuffle, etc. You try to move against your opponent as you would move against a snake. Get as close as you can without being bitten. You try to evoke a response. Your movements are external not internal. Body movements are of four elements:

Dipping

Twisting

Shoulder Roll

Footwork -- step, shuffle, creep, bounce, jump

Leading Center

The way one directs his body, e.g., one can lead with his nose, shoulders, head, etc. The way a person sets his body often reveals what technique the fighter will throw. A shoulder position can conceal the leading center.

Initial Speed

The ability to make quick movements from a relaxed position is essential for kung fu / kenpo excellence. MPH or average speed is of little importance to the fighter. One should be able to move in such a way that his movement either forward or backward is almost undetected. Concentration or will the body to move at maximum speed is an important element in initial speed.

Unpredictability vs. Classical Form

Classical form opts to turn the fighter into a robot; it has no appreciation for differences in strength or size. One needs to be unpredictable in his fighting. If your opponent knows that you are Shotokan and you always lead a lunge punch with a front kick, he can guard well against your attack.

Straight Line vs. Curve Line

You can use a straight line to best a curved line. For example, forefist to beat a roundhouse punch, or ridge hand to beat lunch punch.

Defensive Choices

You can either stand and block, jam, or run.

Initial Speed vs. Combinations

Combinations whose average speed is the same in not as effective as a technique with good initial speed. Even if combinations are used, initial speed must also apply to them.

Faking

Making the opponent think you are going to do something, then see how he reacts, e.g., shoulder fake, hip fake, head fake, etc.

Critical Distance Line

Point where opponent can hit you and can hit him. When you reach this point, you must be "smoking" as two people facing each other nose to nose and emptying their guns point-blank.

Bridging the Gap

How well you can close distance between you and your opponent. The initial independent arm movement can help you bridge the gap. One must always offensively bridge gap. Remember you are moving into critical distance line and to enter this point is always an offensive choice. A hand or foot lead is essential.

Constant Forward Pressure

Keeping the "ON" on your opponent. A heavy psychological commitment is necessary to accomplish this.

Defensive Movement Patterns

Zigzag, move in and out, change postures, etc. If a path is blocked by use of the opponent's feet or hands, change directions. As in football, the quarterback throws where the defenders are not present.

Angle of Attack vs. Technique Variation

Use of same technique in 5 ways - Direct, Indirect, Combination, Broken Rhythm and Binding

Line of Attack

Direction the attack comes e.g., front, side, up, down.

Setups

Make the opponent think you are a certain way when you really are not, e.g., you throw several short back fist to make the opponent think your arm is short then hit with an extended move.

Time Commitment Theory

The initial speed required to complete a movement.

Half Commitment, Full Commitment, Extension Commitment

Understanding the function of the body. Extension for attacking, blocking, faking, etc.

Theory of Broken Rhythm

Be stiff then relax, be quick then slow. Use your rhythm to deceive your opponent.

For a technique to be effective it must:

1. Be explosive

To build explosiveness -- (a) strength and flexibility through exercise, (b) being relaxed.

2. Be deceptive.

To build deceptiveness -- (a) body movement, (b) broken rhythm

Dr. Daniel Kalimaahaaee Pai teaching Professor Glenn C. Wilson

Secrets of White Dragon Kung Fu

Those publicizing the martial arts have, in many instances, given the term "Kung Fu" an inaccurate characterization. The art of Kung Fu has been depicted as a definite style of mayhem and destruction.

Actually the term "Kung Fu" means anything accomplished through time and effort. Hence one who arranges flowers skillfully may be said to practice Kung Fu as well as one who fights successfully.

In practical language, Kung Fu has come to mean the practice of Chinese martial arts. Nevertheless, the range of Kung Fu styles extend from the almost non-existent self defense elements of Tai Chi Chuan to the bellicose Shaolin styles. Therefore Kung Fu can apply to Chinese arts used for exercise and Chinese arts used for fisticuffs.

Some Kung Fu styles are hard and rigid; for example, Hung Gar. Others are soft and flowing; for example Pai Lum, or as it is known in English, White Dragon. The Hung Gar, hard style Kung Fu is very close to karate in its application and theory. One distinct difference between karate and Hung Gar is the emphasis Hung Gar places on the low extreme horse stance, "Sa Pa Mah". The Hung Gar student spends perhaps six months practicing the low horse stance before he graduates into other techniques.

Soft style or White Dragon relies on the fluidity of movement rather than brute strength to achieve its goals. Basically, the White Dragon theory is that one can only move from a position of relaxation to a position of tension. One can not move effectively from a position of tension to a position of tension.

To illustrate this point, tense the muscle in the arm and without relaxing the arm try to punch. Notice how slowly the arm moves.

For the White Dragon style, flowing movement is the height of Kung Fu perfection. Flowing movement is learned through the practice of White Dragon forms such as Flowing Motion, Flowing Water, Golden Fist, etc, and Chi of mind control. Diligent practice of the White Dragon forms leads one away from the human tendency toward tension and stiffness when placed in a stressful situation, such as a physical confrontation.

To free the body from tension also frees the mind. The freedom of the mind to respond from a relaxed state is perhaps the most important goal of the White Dragon style. Most individuals seldom engage in actual physical fights, but psychological confrontation is an everyday state of being. When one's mental state is relaxed, the mind is free to perform to the best of its ability.

To allow the individual to be the very best he can is the end result of the Kung Fu training. With the mental state relieved of so-called "hang-ups", the individual is permitted to respond to each situation without adverse preconceptions weighing over him.

In a fight, the White Dragon student sees only motion generated by the opponent's hands and feet. This motion is not seen in preconceived terms of a punch designed to knock out teeth, but simply a closed hand that speeds toward the body. By not attempting to prejudge any action, the White Dragon exponent is freed to do his best and let what is to happen just happen.

The White Dragon Kung Fu is not necessarily representative of other Kung Fu styles. Each school of Kung Fu must be taken individually in order to understand its secrets.

The Creative Mind

The characteristics of the creative mind are the opposite of those of the reactive mind. The creative mind does not react. It is not dependent on or determined by the stimuli with which it comes into contact. On the contrary, it is active on its own account, functioning spontaneously out of the depths of its own intrinsic nature. Even when initially prompted by something external to itself, it quickly transcends its original point of departure and starts functioning independently.

The creative mind can therefore be said to respond rather than react. Indeed it is capable of transcending conditions altogether. Hence it can be said that whereas the reactive mind is essentially pessimistic (being limited to what is given in immediate experience), the creative mind is profoundly and radically optimistic. Its optimism is not, however, the superficial optimism of the streets, no mere unthinking reaction to, or rationalization of, pleasurable stimuli. By virtue of the very nature of the creative mind, such a reaction would be impossible.

On the contrary, the optimism of the creative mind persists despite unpleasant stimuli, despite conditions unfavorable for optimism, or even when there are no conditions for it at all. The creative mind loves where there is no reason to love, is happy where there is no reason for happiness, creates where there is no possibility of creativity, and in this way "builds heaven in hell's despite."

Not being dependent on any object, the creative mind is essentially non-conditioned. It is independent by nature and functions, therefore, in a perfectly spontaneous manner. When functioning on the highest possible level, at its highest pitch of intensity, the creative mind is identical with the unconditioned, that is to say, it coincides with absolute mind. Being non-conditioned, or unconditioned, the creative mind is free. Indeed it is freedom itself. It's also original in the true sense of the term, being characterized by ceaseless productivity. This productivity is not necessarily artistic, literary, or musical, even though the painting, the poem, and the symphony are admittedly among its most strikingly adequate manifestations. Moreover, just as the creative mind does not necessarily find expression in "works of art," so what are traditionally called "works of art" are not necessarily all expressions of the creative mind. Imitative and lacking true originality, some of them are more likely to be mechanical products of the reactive mind.

Outside the sphere of the fine arts, the creative finds expression in productive personal relations, as when through the emotional positiveness others become more emotionally positive, or as when through the intensity of the their mutual awareness two or more people reach our towards, and together, experience a dimension of being greater and more inclusive than their separate individualities.

In these and similar cases the creative mind is productive, in the sense of contributing to the increase in the world of the sum total of positive emotion, of higher states of being and consciousness. Finally, as just indicated, the creative mind is, above all, the aware mind. Being aware, or rather, being awareness of itself, the creative mind is also intensely and radiantly alive. The creative person, as one in whom the creative mind manifests itself may be called, is not only more aware than the reactive person, but is possessed of a far greater vitality. This vitality is not just animal high spirits, or emotional exuberance, much less still mere intellectual energy or the compulsive urgency of egotistic volition. Where such expressions are permissible, one might say it is the spirit of life itself rising like a fountain from the infinite depths of existence, and vivifying, through the creative person, all with whom it comes into contact.

White Fire Dragon Warrior

When you fight what you cannot understand is when you achieve the fear of getting hurt. Once you can absorb that hurt feeling, everything will become easier.

In the way of the White Dragon, we learn to read a person - not judge them, but read them to see what is in their innermost self. Try to see how they will react to you.

White Dragon people are honorable, courteous, and humble before all else. To be a true White Dragon is to have confidence enough in your knowledge that you don't have to tell people what you are. They should be able to tell just by watching and listening to you. Being overly confident of your knowledge is not a way of the White Dragon. If you are a true White Dragon, you know you are great and you should know it so deeply that you don't have to put it in someone's ear. Let them make up their own and decide if you are what you claim you are. If you are good don't say it - but be ready to prove it if the time arises.

By Great Grandmaster Dr. Daniel Kalimaahaaee 'Kane' Pai

Knowing The Angles

Our Pai Lum System has been blessed with many philosophies and theories. All of these have been tested time and again in actual combat and have proven to be worthy of being called Pai Lum. Picking one to write about is not an easy task. Like much of our art you will find that separating theories from each other is not an easy thing to do. Pai Lum is a complex art! That is why the numbers of true masters is not great.

Today I wish to look into the use of angles for evasion. The use of angles is something that can be found at the very root of our system. Angles are used in the evasion of attacks as well as in the delivery of counterstrikes. We all know that we train in a martial art. So, at some point we are introduced to the fact that somebody is going to attack us. This is where our use of the basics we learn in class with certain theories (angles in this case) work together.

Using angles is not hard or a mystical secret! The first point that everyone must learn is: know your surroundings! An awareness of the area around you gives you the ability to use what you have learned. If an attack, let's say a punch to the face, is coming from the front we know that our first reaction is to neutralize this immediate threat. Keeping with today's subject of using angles we can see many ways to neutralize the punch. Not only can we step to evade this threat, but it also gives us an advantage by positioning ourselves so we can maximize our counter. Also, different types of blocks used in conjunction with stepping further aid us in setting up our opponent for defeat.

Pai Lum has an extensive arsenal of stances and techniques to choose from. The student starts learning these from their first day of training. Some are at the basic core of our style, the square horse stance for example. Others, like the monkey stance, can be found as a student progresses through the rank system. The same holds true for blocks! Whether it is a gong chuan or a blowing windmill block it will be found in the training.

The use of an angle for evading an attack is comprised of us stepping into a certain stance in a given direction that will take the intended target out of the path or range of the attack. This can, but does not have to be, coupled with a block. An example of this could be stepping straight to the rear into a longbow stance. This will move your center back out of range of the strike. Another example, one using a block, is stepping out to the side into a square horse stance and at the same time doing an outward gong chuan block.

These examples are using straight angles. First though, we must understand the angles and what we are describing. The use of a diagram can help visualize these.

As you can see I listed on the diagram both the compass points and the degrees. People find it easier to use one or the other or maybe even relating the movements to the numbers on the face of a clock. Either is acceptable as long as we remember to correlate the angles correctly.

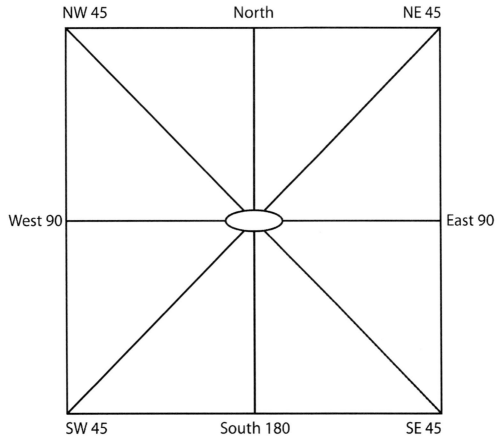

For the continuity of his article I will refer to the points of the compass. We will start at the center facing north as a rule.

If we step straight back to the south with either foot into a longbow stance we take the target back out of range of the punch. The down side of this is that we then have to return into his range to counter.

We also can step out to either side into a square horse stance and this removes the target from the direct path of the punch. You must, however, remember that if you step to the inside of his zone, that is if he punches with a right punch and you step out to your right he may still be in range with his left hand. If you wish to do this it is fine, just remember that you are in such a position. One possible scenario could be to do an outward gong chuan block with and punch with the right at the same time.

Another way is to utilize the 45° angles. These angles when used with the right stances and techniques will lead to a formidable arsenal. Stepping forward or back at this angle can be done with either foot. A step out forward with the left foot at a 45° to the NW will take the attackers intended target to the side and forward where his punch will be ineffective. If this step is used in conjunction with a blocking technique like blowing windmill then you will end up behind him on his right side. A quick pivot into a square horse to the NE or back into a long bow in the opposite direction (SE) will put you in position to deliver a multitude of different techniques.

So far what I have discussed is using basic stances and stepping. As a student progresses and is exposed to more complex techniques of course there are more complex stepping patterns that can be integrated into his training. Monkey and Dragon are two that utilize angular stepping in conjunction with twisting and spinning to gain the advantage over the opponent. There are many stepping combinations that can be used. Linear, circular, angular, or putting any combination together is part of what makes this so great.

This is only an introduction into a wonderful theory. If you have any questions, and I hope that this does cause you to have many, asking your teacher is always a good thing! The only dumb question is the one that goes unasked.

I know that some of what I have been saying will be obvious to some that have been training longer, but this is aimed at the newer, younger students that haven't been exposed yet. As students progress hopefully they will keep this in mind.

Just a hint, look at your fist sets and much of what I have just said you will see!

The Art of Training like a True Warrior!

Train first with the Mind;

Clear in thought and purpose, focused on your actions Visualizing the correct techniques, Until thought and action become one!

Train secondly with the Body;

Posture straight and true, Stances aligned and deep Completing techniques with power and speed, Building the strength up and delivering it to it target!

Train thirdly with the Heart;

Passion and Desire for our art,

Tempered with Compassion and Loyalty.

Intensity focused on the task. The Heart, Home to the Spirit,

"The Warrior Spirit!!"

Ego

Regard yourself too highly; the only open path is down. Thinking yourself unworthy, you will be proven wrong. Keep yourself to the mid ground; one can grow with the good and the bad!

The Circle

On the circle of life there is no high or low, Just different points from which to observe and learn.

The Young

Look around the world shows how to care for ones young, Nurture with compassion, Feed with knowledge, Guide with discipline!

The Teacher

The true teacher hold fast to his students; To take this path you put them first, Wisdom, Knowledge, Their growth is your responsibility!

Family

Is Family just a group of close blood relatives? Some may think so. Family truly has no bounds, not blood, not color, not religion. Family is a group brought together by a common cause and bound by values and compassion for each other. A Families worth is seen in the integrity of its members!

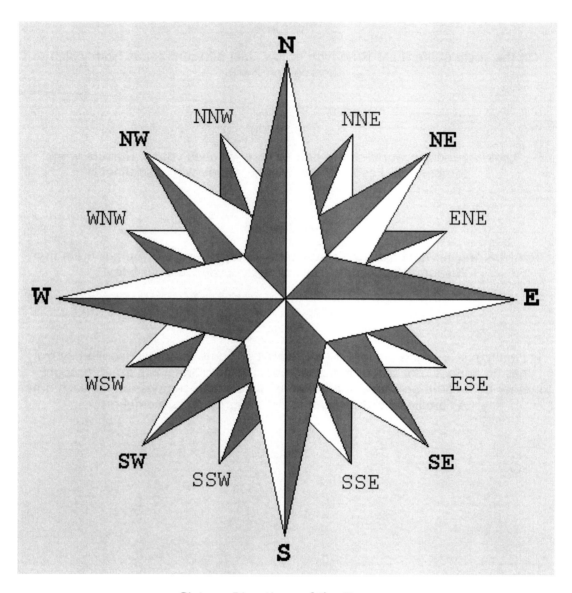

Sixteen Directions of the Dragon

Stances

Stances are the very foundation that any Martial Art is built upon. A student will spend hours upon hours training in low powerful stances. This builds the legs to a higher level of strength and endurance as well as creates an overwhelming weapon.

Proper stance is vital to the practitioner for several reasons. Stability, power, diversity in movement and ultimately speed and accuracy of technique start at the ground. Yes, it is drummed into the head of every Bok Leen Pai Kenpo practitioner, stance – posture – technique.

The varied stances fall into two basic categories, stationary or transitionary. In the stationary stance the practitioner locks into a powerful stance that holds their ground or territory at all cost. The work done during the training of the stationary stance insures that the student will have legs of iron.

The transitionary stance will be applied while the practitioner is traveling across the floor from one movement to another. These stances will be lighter and require more agility and dexterity. Strikes are executed successfully from both of these stances.

The distance between the practitioner and their attacker is extremely important and will ultimately determine which stance is chosen. A common gauge for determining stance and counter is called 'leg length'. At this distance one may be able to calculate the attack and respond successfully with a barrage of counter attacks. This is also called the 'safe circle'.

A good and proper stance allow a practitioner to prepare for any encounter. One will utilize their 'calmness of mind' as well as their breathing to overcome adversity. They will stabilize, regulate, control and deliver a successful story rather it is in combat or expression. The stance is the beginning of all stories told within the Martial Arts.

Some of the Stances executed in Bok Leen Pai Kenpo:

Square Horse

Long Bow

Short Bow

Side Horse

Scissors

Coiled Snake

One Knee Set

Cat

Crane

Pigeon

Twisting Horse

Sitting Buddha

Crossed Leg Buddha

Break

Ready

Neutral

Blocks

Blocks are the predecessor to all of one's counter strikes. It is said that "if do not block successfully, you do not have the luxury of countering". Thus, you will fail in your encounter! Blocks are used to disrupt the attacker, misdirect the assault, defuse and neutralize their energy, discourage their meaning, dampen their spirit and ultimately crush or cut their attack to nothing! Yes, blocking is one of the most important physical and philosophical expressions we can use on an attacker.

A basic theory in Bok Leen Pai Kenpo is to 'deal with the immediate threat'. All attacks have what is taught as the two 'Ds', direction and degree. It is common to apply the theory of 'evade and strike' to an attacker's assault. This is determined by ones own speed, timing, angle of direction and technique chosen. Displacing the attacker's force becomes common practice and proves to be a very successful formula of execution.

Vertical, circular and force utilization are the three basic exercises and theories of countering. Mastering the understanding of these basic yet, at times, complex theories is a must. Only through proper instruction may the student understand the depth of this training. This mastering is most important to the success of any martial encounter. An in depth understanding and proper training will teach the practitioner that the formula utilizing: attack force, component of angle and direction, speed –vs- divergent force, blocking energy, defusing technique, rapid fire repetition and technical intent, will ultimately tell the story of one's successful battle!

Some of the Blocks executed in Bok Leen Pai Kenpo:

Upward Gong Chuan

Inward Gong Chuan

Outward Gong Chuan

Downward Gong Chuan

Upward Yuen Chuan

Inward Yuen Chuan

Outward Yuen Chuan

Downward Yuen Chuan

Upward Crane Crossing Wings
Gong Chuan

Downward Crane Crossing
Wings Gong Chuan

Upward Crane Crossing
Wings Yuen Chuan

Downward Crane Crossing
Wings Yuen Chuan

Twin Pines

Twin Outward Wings
Gong Chuan

Twin Outward Wings
Yuen Chuan

Cranes Head

Cranes Beak

Hammer Fists

Retreating Elbow

Double Inward Crane
Wings Snaps

Punches/Strikes

The punches and hand strikes of Bok Leen Pai Kenpo encompass approximately eighty percent of a practitioners arsenal. It is said that the first strike may knock out the would be attacker, the other six strikes are merely icing on the cake. Yes, an attacker may be struck six times before they hit the ground. This is due to the lightening speed and vast arsenal that the artist posses due to their traditional training.

It is taught in Bok Leen Pai Kenpo that strikes should never be initiated as an offensive attack. The philosophy is to have the most powerful and successful defensive techniques possible. This state of mind supports a peaceful environment coupled with a very successful 'counterattack' mindset.

Strikes are aimed a specific weak spots and pressure points in the body. Depending on the attack, the response will be delivered with certain power, speed, rhythm and technique. These four virtues driven by one's intent and purpose will equal the ultimate outcome. The hand techniques of Bok Leen Pai Kenpo are some of the most respected and feared of any martial art practiced to date!

Some of the Hand Strikes executed in Bok Leen Pai Kenpo:

Reverse Ram's Head

Sun Fist

Back Knuckle

Hammer Fist

Twin Ram's Head

Upper Cut

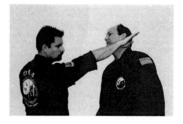

Outside Crane's Wing

Inside Crane's Wing

Twin Inside Crane Wings

Knife Hands

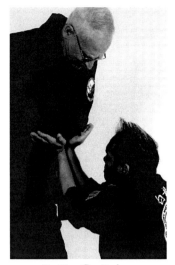

Butterfly Palms

Tiger Claw

Pecking Crane's Beak

Twin Ram's Head

Leopard's Paw

Spear Hand

Falcon Claw

Dragon's Head

Fanning The Clouds

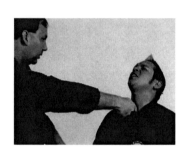

Eye Of The Phoenix

Immortal Man Points
The Way

Twin Dragons Searching
For The Pearls

White Snake Hand

Praying Mantis

Chapter 5
Shaolin Cutting Fists

Shaolin Cutting Series

Many fighting theories have evolved throughout the diverse and expansive martial arts history of China. The legacy of fighting techniques and styles has been compiled by generations of skilled warriors who drew from personal combat experiences. The theories and formulas generated by such activity were employed in combat by the warrior, who believed that his technique and style would be superior on the battlefield. The warrior would train diligently and thoroughly to master each technique. The warrior could not afford failure; the price for failure was usually death. The warrior's training would form the basis for a unique fighting style, the worth of which would ultimately be proven on the field of combat.

One of the by-products of this constant development was the White Dragon / Pai Lum system and its highly effective series of cutting punches and kicks. This highly guarded and effective fighting theories are at the very center core of Pai Lum Taos two external disciplines - Bok Leen Pai Kenpo and Pai Te Lung Kung Fu. The cutting series strikes to a target using vertical, horizontal, and circular motions. Distinguishing the cutting series from other theories and formulas are its unique composition of linear and circular striking, which are utilized within the implementation of every move.

Although the technique is endowed with power and explosiveness, it is the penetration of the cutting punch or kick that highlights its significance. The technique is thrown into the target, but does not stop at it; instead, it cuts through the target. Such devastating penetration and diffusion makes these techniques among the most effective and deadly in the martial arts repertoire.

Cutting punches developed from an evolution of fighting styles. Borrowing from the strengths of both Northern and Southern kung-fu, the cutting punch emerged as a powerful combination of motion-generated power and explosive short-range combat.

The Northern style is known for its mobile stances and long-range striking. The Southern style enveloped a belief in short-range explosiveness into a target. The Northern style developed sinew strength and power through movement. The Southern style practiced powerful explosion into the target area. From a blending of motion and explosion, the cutting punch emulated venerable qualities of both styles.

The cutting punches employ both gong (hard) and yuen (soft) theories and applications of Pai Lum Tao Kenpo and martial arts in general. They use either a basic shoulder whipping motion or a figure-eight pattern in which are made a continuous series of punches. The cutting punches and kicks are delivered quickly, often many times a second in a rapid fire type of delivery, to overwhelm an opponent. This speedy delivery will interrupt the thinking and reacting process of the opponent.

The momentum of the cutting punch finds its basis in strong, solid stance work. From the toe, the energy moves into the calf, travels up the thigh, is reinforced by the hip, surges through the waist, shoots up the back, travels into the shoulder, elbow and wrist, and culminates in the fist. The hand technique strikes into and through the target. During the movement, the air should travel from the body via the mouth, directly matching the physical motion of the technique.

As the cutting series is executed, the body should be relaxed, yet firm: tight muscles or joints should be avoided, as this restricts energy flow, and interferes with sinew and/or muscle movement vital to the proper execution of this technique. Relaxation is necessary to allow the body to express the whipping motion required to guide the path of the punch or kick. Stiff, tense motion contradicts the fluidity and adaptability this technique demands.

The cutting series of punches utilizes linear and circular motions combined into one continuous, fluid movement. Different parts of the hand may be used to transform this energy into unique and effective strikes, Pin chuan (flat punch, as in a ram's head punch) cuts with the fore knuckles, driving directly into and then ripping through the target. Basically, the punch penetrates a few inches into the target with a linear motion and then cuts through with a continued circular motion, which results in the hand either being chambered at the body or continuing in the opposite direction (as in a series of cutting punches).

Other hand positions include:

- Li chuan (vertical fist, as in sunfist);

- Fan sou chuan (reverse hand strike);

- Bon chuan (backfist);

- Pie chuan (palm slap);

- Wye hen sou (elbow/forearm);

- Sou den (elbow strike)

- Hen chie (chopping wing).

The system of cutting techniques also includes a number of cutting kicks. These can be further distinguished into a subcategory of jumping cutting kicks. Utilizing relaxed, fluid motion focussed on penetration also applies to the kicks. Among the kicks are:

- Ti twe (front toe)

- Teng twe (heel strike)

- Shi ding (knee strike)

- Wye bie (sweeping/crescent)

- Nei bie (sweeping/crescent)

- Tse tie (side)

The two major jumping kicks are tiao teng twe, which strikes with the heel, and tiao hou teng twe, a rear/jumping spin kick.

Some of these techniques may be recognizable by name as being practiced elsewhere in the martial arts: the distinction is that these techniques are executed in a unique manner. The cutting punches and cutting kicks penetrate and cut through the target as a single execution.

In Shaolin chuan fa cutting techniques, there is no adjustment of the hand or body in reaction to the target. There is a designated target, but should that target move, the technique is designed to smash and destroy whatever lies in its path.

Serious conditioning of the body and training of the mind is required before these techniques can be properly mastered. Solid stance-work and chi kung breathing methods also must already be firmly established before beginning the complete range of cutting technique training.

Before the first true technique is taught, the student must concentrate on learning proper breathing and acquiring an understanding of the techniques. The techniques are then practiced against the heavy bag, where penetration and cutting through the target arc established. Finally, the techniques are worked in two-man sets, with body padding serving to absorb the impact of the punch. These two-man sets polish the cutting technique, and teach the student how to properly take the cutting punch or kick. This training is supervised by qualified instructors to assure that injuries are kept to a minimum.

Iron-palm training works in conjunction with cutting punch training. Iron palm serves to make the hands tough and conditioned, necessary for the appropriate application of the cutting punch. The iron-palm training centers on working a variety of set punches into a bag or iron pellets or stones. This repeated, intense work builds and conditions the hands so more power and penetration might be derived from each technique. Dit da jow is employed to prevent injury to the iron-palm practitioner while training in this strenuous exercise.

In spite of the extreme lethality of these techniques, very few martial artist outside rural areas of China have ever received this astonishing training and knowledge. To ever have a solid understanding of the 'cutting' concepts or theories one must train with an authorized instructor or injury will surely come about. Although once practiced only behind closed doors, the cutting punch and kicking series are available through a few instructors of Pai Lum Tao and traditional Shaolin schools.

Chapter 6
Brutal Takedowns

Brutal Takedowns

For those unfortunate people who choose to stand toe to toe with a "Bok Leen Pai practitioner", the confrontation will be decided at the hands and feet of the Pai Lum Tao practitioner instructed in the utilization of brutal takedowns.

If a student is a product of his teacher, then a master's art is truly a reflection of his life. Grandmaster Daniel Kane Pai devoted his life to not only mastering the art of Pai Lum (frequently referred to as the white dragon system), but proving and educating the world to its effectiveness.

Pai Lum is an art renowned for its well-rounded arsenal with one of its most effective attributes being its brutal takedowns. During his heyday many practitioners found themselves at Grandmaster Pai's mercy when the powerful Hawaiian rendered his opponent helpless with the execution of these brutal takedowns. These takedowns were the result of a natural process of evolution of the arts taught within his family and the influences of his Chinese, Hawaiian and Okinawan tutelage. The illumination of Shorinji Kempo, Judo, Ju Jitsu, Shuai chiao and wrestling commingled into the very heart of his devastating fighting style.

Fortunate Few

These takedowns were reflected throughout his teachings and instilled in the many who chose to train in his system of martial arts. Those fortunate enough to be at the receiving end of grandmaster's flawless takedowns not only understood the rigors of being called "white dragons", but soon found of which legends are made. Only after many hours of intense training were the dragons allowed to lick their wounds and one day come to the realization of what the master was trying to teach, an art that "must work, not play".

Dr. Pai made sure that all aspects of the Pai Lum system were going to work when the time came for the practitioner to call upon the skill. He often said. "If it doesn't work, its no damn good, and it isn't Pai Lum." This statement does not only pertain to Pai Lum's brutal takedowns, but to every aspect taught within this system.

The White Dragon system is truly a product of a lifelong devotion and a love of martial arts. Dr. Pai gives credit for his art's effectiveness and applicability to his early judo and kempo training in Hawaii, as well as the vast arsenal of Shuai chiao and chin na found in the various family styles within the white dragon system.

Judo gives the practitioner a strong foundation in grappling and throwing techniques, while kempo contributes rapid-fire, no-nonsense street fighting techniques. Shuai chiao, being the mother of all grappling arts, aids the practitioner in more fine-tuned trapping and jointlock techniques developed on the principle that throwing an opponent to the ground proved to be a quick and effective way to end a confrontation.

These techniques are complemented by a pinpoint nerve manipulating system known as chin na, an art that concentrates on the more than 200 pressure points found throughout the body.

Pai Lum Tao Philosophy

The merging of these various styles proved to mesh well with the Pai Lum philosophy of utilizing powerful punches and kicks to immobilize an attacker and gain complete control of the confrontation with a savage takedown. Once the attacker is helpless on the ground regardless of the combination used, the practitioner would have ample time to escape, detain, or take further action as needed.

The unique blend of movements within the Pai Lum Tao system ensures that there are no set offensive or defensive techniques. Once an attack is initiated, the Pai Lum Tao practitioner would react with blinding speed utilizing every block as a strike and every strike as a block, with the formula "follow the source back and you will find the target".

This allows the practitioner a no-nonsense reaction to the attack, keeping in mind that one should alleviate the problem fully. The combination of blocking, punching, kicking and takedown, then strike again proves to he a successful formula for self-defense.

Along with awesome speed and accuracy of the techniques, utilization of maximum waist whipping enables the Pai Lum Tao practitioner an effortless takedown and weaves a pattern of magical motion. This motion is unleashed with a flurry of circular, straight, or trapping techniques which explode so rapidly that the opponent has been permanently affixed to the floor by a brutal takedown before he realizes what has taken place. Incorporating a combination of thrusts, traps, locks, pressure points, and throws gives the practitioner a loaded arsenal to achieve maximum results with minimal effort.

Art of Takedowns

Because most fighters feel more comfortable rooted to the ground, which can make them an immovable force, the White Dragon practitioner is schooled in the art of takedowns to ensure his command of even the most powerful and aggressive attackers. The effectiveness of takedowns, however, does not require great feats of strength; they are based on medical and scientific principles of motion which are applied to the attacker's muscles, joints, or the pressure points found throughout the body. The motion initiated by the attacker is redirected by the Pai Lum Tao practitioner resulting in a two-pronged effect; the attacker losing his rooting followed immediately by impact.

Ground impact can cause a range in injury level from slight to severe and may result in fainting, paralyzing, or even death. With a well-rounded arsenal of over 900 techniques to blend with hard or soft movements they can be either offensive or defensive, the Pai Lum Tao student is confident in his situation knowing that his teachings have covered all possible avenues.

This incorporates not only the physical, but the mental aspects of the system; Pai Lum Tao is a thinking art and produces intelligent martial artists. This assures that when the time comes for the Pai Lum Tao practitioner to call upon their skills, they will react without hesitation. This is a priceless quality, as anyone who has had to put their skills to the test will substantiate.

Most confrontations are decided within the first few seconds, and for those unfortunate people who choose to stand toe to toe with a "white dragon", the confrontation will he decided even quicker, at the hands and feet of the Bok Leen Pai practitioner instructed in the utilization of brutal takedowns.

'Brutal Takedowns'

Fist Sets

(A)

1 – Rich Wilson prepares for encounter by setting in double Gong Chuan fighting stance while Hilda Wilson sets in traditional Gong Yuen Chuan Fa battle form posture

2 - Rich strikes out with a spear hand while Hilda intercepts and performs the rising branch technique snapping the arm at the elbow

3 – Hilda executes a traditional Bok Leen Pai Kenpo overhead wrist throw slamming the attacker to the ground

4 – Hilda continues to snap the wrist while delivering a traditional Chinese cutting punch to the ribs

(A) - 1

(A) - 2

(A) - 3

(A) - 4

(B)

1 – Jim Stone sets in traditional Kenpo Crane extends wings stance while Glenn Wilson prepares in Gong Yuen Chuan Fa classical fighting stance

2 – Stone attacks with a right front kick while Wilson blocks with a downward cross wing pattern

3 – Wilson captures the attacking leg while delivering a 'Tigers Mouth' to the throat and hooking the supporting leg for the takedown

4 – Wilson maintains a grab on the attacker's leg while stomping the groin

(B) - 1

(B) - 2

(B) - 3

(B) - 4

(C)

1 – Bryan Naegele prepares for conflict in a double Gong Chuan stance while Glenn Wilson sets in a Gong Yuen Crane posture

2 – Naegele attacks with a left lunging punch while Wilson performs 'Cat plays with ball' routine

3 – Wilson performs a traditional Bok Leen Pai Kenpo 'Casting the net' takedown

4 – Wilson maintains control of attackers arm while delivering a sun fist to the temple

(C) - 1   (C) - 2

(C) - 3   (C) - 4

Chapter 7
Explosive Short Wings

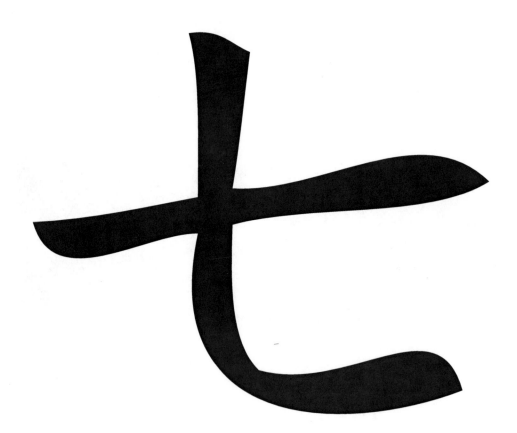

Explosive Short Wings

There are as many "favorite techniques" as there are martial arts styles and martial artists. The techniques become trademarks of your "way of execution". Techniques are varied depending on what the style may dictate as far as its philosophies as well as the individual artist's performance. The artist's performance will more than likely be determined by size, strength, speed, and total understanding of "fighting formulas" and their ability to execute them.

The legendary late grandmaster of Pai Lum Tao, Daniel Kane Pai, was renowned for his short-range combat and few could execute its techniques as smoothly and as effectively. With his trademark "short wing" moves, he could drop an opponent with a blink of an eye or shatter a thousand pounds of ice while a sea of cameras flashed throughout the stadium. Yes, the short wings of Pai Lum Tao have survived the test of time through out the martial arts development and evolution and have proven to be as effective an arsenal as any practiced today.

Where To Start

Students begin with the seven star training of arm conditioning. Together, two students will strike each other's forearms, biceps, triceps and hands to prepare them for the "initial contact" strike. Striking air may serve to train other areas of one's arsenal, but it does nothing to prepare the eager student for the contact that inevitably will occur in a confrontation.

The hands are the extremities of the wing and for many practitioners, the most used. Striking open hands together "palm and back", they will slap firmly but not as hard as possible. This creates a format of rhythm and conditioning for the outer most part of the wing. This exercise will be done thousands of times until it becomes natural. Then from a disciplined stance, inside low and high wings (forearms) will strike, followed by outside techniques and finally linear and horizontal attacks.

Once the practitioner has made his box set proficient he will move to the next step— "armor training", where a partner allows light blows to the body's "non-vital areas" for conditioning of the receivers, as well as realistic targetry for the executor. This aspect of Pai Lum Tao training has proven most beneficial for real-life understanding. In many cases, it's the difference between playing tackle football and engaging in a playful game of two-handed touch. Care must always be taken to work safely from the fingers to the elbow of the short wings.

Soaking the hands with traditional dragon dit da jow will prepare the students for contact. Vigorous conditioning must become a part of one's regular routine; the artist who one day deals with real hard contact quickly discovers the head can be harder than the hand. This so many times has resulted in the unexpecting practitioner acquiring broken bones in the hands and arms, a shocking reality with which to deal.

A must are thousands of carefully executed strikes to the hard pad "makiwara", bean and stone bag as well as the traditional heavy bay. The student begins with a ritual of "placement punching." He punches to the target to allow the hand, arm and elbow to receive the return shock of the strike. When proficient he then begins to penetrate mentally and physically into the target area. This allows a mental confidence to build as the body conditions itself for the inevitable encounter.

The Essence Of All Wings

The elbow of the short wing is considered the most lethal. From streetfighting to Muay Thai boxing, when one is in really tight with his opponent the elbow becomes the shotgun of the short wings. It explodes with lightning speed and destroys everything in its path. The array of techniques begin with the horizontal—inward then outward; the vertical-— rising and dropping; and then the corner sets of the four 45-degree angle strikes. This octagon pattern is the basis of Pai Lum Tao's zone directions. Within two feet, it is virtually impossible to stop. Even if the opponent stops the short wing elbow it will surely damage the blocking area. That will eventually lead to a critical path to the target zone. Hence, the attacker is out.

Body range is truly the success or failure of one's assault. Knowing the depth factor involved at time of engagement will trigger the correct response by the trained practitioner. That will be the moment of truth—the time when the portion of the short wing that will be used to strike will be determined. The triceps, elbow, forearm, hand blade, palm or claw will become a utensil of destruction. Knowing the range of the assault, the transition "follow-up" desired, and the necessary outcome will instantaneously determine which utensil is called.

Understanding the tool to be used in the encounter is critical. If the circumstances dictate that one has the choice, it should be among poke, claw, cut or crush from the hand or a whip, snap or drive of the forearm/elbow. Understanding what the executioner wants as a result of the technique is critical. All these techniques are effective in their own right, yet used at the wrong time or place can very well limit their effectiveness. The variables include distance, depth of technique, body alignment, surrounding conditions, type of attack you are facing, and your proficiency.

Reflexology becomes your guide— knowing what to throw, when to throw it and where it will land. Such combinations as covering, penetrating, transition, power, depth, rhythm, focus and alertness determine success or failure. Once fusing these combinations into a rhythmic pattern has been achieved, the Pai Lum Tao practitioner is well on his way to understanding the true philosophies of Bok Leen Pai Kenpo and Pai Te Lung Kung Fu.

To understand targetry, the Pai Lum Tao student conditions himself from his early training to follow specific formulas. First he learns to visualize, focus, then execute; the best technique in the world is useless if it misses its target. Furthermore, before you get the luxury of the next technique the previous one must have been successful.

Moving targets provide a much greater challenge to the attacker. This is where rhythm and designated pattern work become essential. You must understand the natural flow of motion, whether it is yours or your opponent's.

Power From The Ground

To appreciate the benefits of Pai Lum's unique program, the formula of stance, posture and technique are endlessly drilled. In Pai Lum Tao the deliverance is from the ground up. This maximizes power, flow and penetration.

With continuous training one develops the intuition of decision. The decision is one of instantaneous thought and reaction. A blinding response to an attacker's assault is the key to success—which may be the difference between victory or defeat, life or death. One must have full confidence in the teachings of his particular style.

Though we practice our arts for self-esteem, self-confidence, self-respect and most assuredly, self-defense, we must understand the key meaning of self. As practitioners we are the ones who are learning the ancient ways and bringing them ever so quickly into the 21st century. An art proven through time will survive change, challenge and scrutiny. For it has been written, "No road is as long or filled with as many obstacles as the one traveled by Chinese boxers."

As we pass these lethal techniques and philosophies on to the next generation of martial artists, keep in mind there are few techniques in the martial arsenal as lethal as the short wings of Pai Lum Tao.

Elbow Sequence

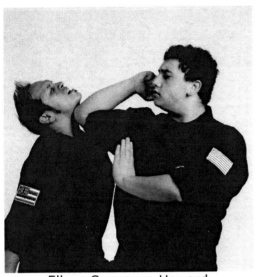

Elbow Sequence Upward

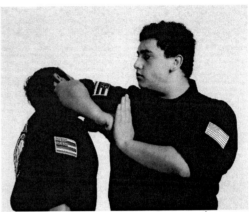

Elbow Sequence Outward

Elbow Sequence Inward

Elbow Sequence Downward

Chapter 8
Lethal Legs

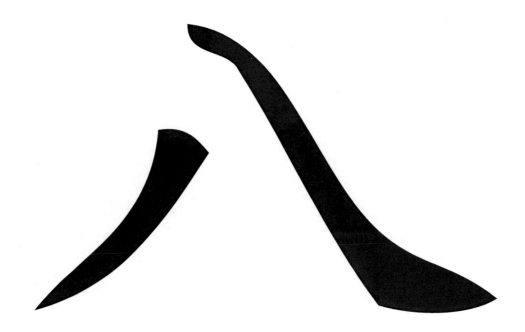

Lethal Legs

The "fist law" has many faces and natures to it. In their diversity kenpo disciplines find similarities. Some prefer a harder execution —while others favor a softer deliverance. The majority of Kenpo disciplines prefer to mix these two natures. A rhythmic deliverance of techniques, some hard and some soft are played out developing a very beautiful lethal system of martial arts.

You will find a certain loyalty among Kenpo practitioners toward their particular discipline of kenpo and kenpo in general. Among such unique systems of Kenpo as Kosho, Shoreiryu, Kajukenbo, Shaolin Kenpo, Chinese Kenpo, Shorinji, Won Hop Kuen Do, American Kenpo, Kara-ho, and Tracy's kenpo, lies a secretive and time-proven system of Kenpo — Bok Leen Pai.

Bok Leen Pai, the "White Lotus Family" system of martial arts, is a blend of the disciplines of the Byakurenji Temple training and the Pai Family chuan fa. This blend took place in the early 1900s thanks to Sijo Pai Po Fong. The rigorous, and at times brutal, training of the Byakurenji set the foundation of Pai Lum Tao training in general. With the test of time, a style or system will ultimately be as good as the teachers that promote it. Bok Leen Pai's history tells who and what they are. Bok Leen Pai is a Kenpo system recognized for its hand speed, kicking power and traditional martial arts values.

Where Are The Kicks?

Traditionally, Bok Leen Pai Kenpo is about 75 percent hands and 25 percent feet. Stories told of the hand techniques of Bok Leen Pai are well earned. Don't concentrate too much, however, on those mystical hand movements or you won't see the Bok Leen Pai's thunderous kicks.

Kicks are targeted to the rib cage and down. The execution of the kick is to cut, crush or disrupt. Hidden behind the barrage of intricate hand techniques are lethal and sometimes seemingly invisible leg strikes.

Key factors such as power, speed, conditioning and deliverance are the ingredients of success. Bok Leen Pai kicks are used to lead the barrage, break down the root, dislodge weight distribution, intercept assaulting techniques, trap and disorient, as well as finish a confrontation with crushing and slicing techniques that penetrate and cut through the attack.

Kicks are delivered with extreme power and execution, and feature in-depth penetration to pinpoint target areas. Power kicks begin with hours of slow, disciplined kick execution. Kicks are done in an easy isometric fashion until the proper muscles, tendons and ligaments are properly conditioned One then begins to develop power with 'the bag". This entails starting with drills into sawdust and sandbags. The power developed through sandbag training is incredible. It is not uncommon for a Pai Lum Tao practitioner to shatter the leg of a wooden dummy in half with a shin strike.

Some of the basic standards for Bok Leen Pai Kenpo kicking are:

- Never leave the groin exposed;

- Shift weight to the supporting leg prior to the kick;

- Exhale when kicking, matching the breath with the kicks:

- Perform kicks to the ribs and mid section down;

- Kick to, into, then through the targeted area;

- Relax the body for maximum Chi flow;

- Dragon waist whipping for maximum penetration and power;

- Keep supporting leg 'foot' flat on the ground;

- Kicks should always quickly retract to the original position;

- Chop the opponent's base or foundation

- Whipping and snapping must be mastered.

Thousands of kicks will be executed to the air in front of the mirror partner. This helps the kick flow freely and relaxed. This modern form of training has proven its worth many times over. Speed can only be mastered in one's kicks when the body relaxed. Proper breathing patterns must be practiced to relieve the body of stress and tension. The kick should explode from a set position to maximum penetration in the blink of an eye.

Leg strikes such as monk's spade, knife edge, roundhouse, wheel, front snap and side heel are popular within the leg striking series. These Bok Leen Pai Kenpo leg strikes are unyielding in their execution. They have been called deceptive, distracting, frustrating, confusing, invisible, vicious and always lethal.

Front Snap   Front Stomp   Side Heel

Knife

Rear

Chopping Axe

Inside Crescent Moon

Roundhouse

Outside Crescent Moon

Wheel

Hook

Monks Spade

Chicken

Knee Sequence Wheel

Knee Sequence Vertical

Knee Sequence
Dropping

Iron Broom

Rising Earth

Chapter 9
The Crushing Iron Hand

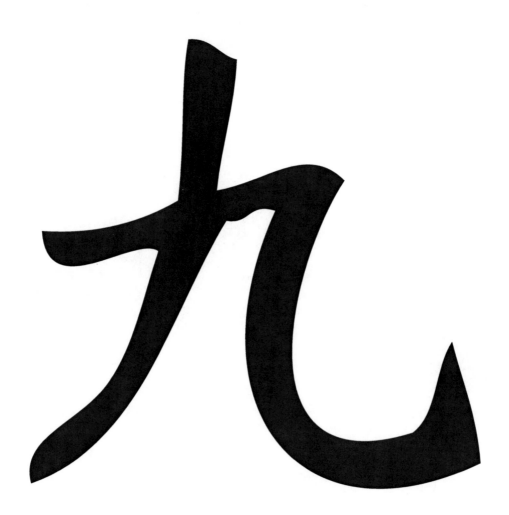

The Crushing Iron Hand

Daniel Kane Pai was definitely one of the most respected and feared fighters of his time, as well as a renowned master of the iron hand techniques and training. His Iron Hand secrets were one of the most prized trainings found with in Pai Lum Tao – Bok Leen Pai Kenpo and Pai Te Lung Kung Fu!

He was highly respected for his ice-breaking demonstrations, which drew many top martial artists to him for lessons. This legendary Grand Master taught several American martial artists only some of the iron hand training, but as all great visionaries, he saved the best for a handful of his loyal students and disciples.

Iron hand training is one of the segments of training found within the iron body discipline of Pai Lum Tao. This type of training takes dedication and determination to maintain. The student develops his internal chi training to work perfectly with the external training. Iron body training takes many years to develop. The hand/fist training is referred to in many systems as iron palm. Pai Lum Tao teaches formulas that make the area from the wrist to the fingertips as strong as iron.

Of the many training strikes used on a training bag, the most prominent are the heel palm, crane's beak, palm of hand, backhand, willow palm and tiger claw.

External Training

Iron hand training is divided into external and internal exercises. External exercises consist of the "pounding road" theories of training. At the very core of training is striking hard surfaces while using different hand strikes. The hand strikes are determined based on the level of proficiency of the student. Students often measure their level based on how long it takes to execute a certain number of strikes on the training bag.

The grueling training begins after the proper application of dit da jow herbal medicine, which is used to preserve and protect the hand. Under the eye of a certified instructor, the student will begin what is known as the pounding road. This is the road that all iron hand students will travel enthusiastically.

Massaging the hands with a special dit dot jow is a vital section of iron hand training. The use of herbal medicine aids in preventing severe deformity of the hands, enhances blood flow, heals damaged areas and speeds up the recovery process. Another function of dit da jow is to assist chi flow to the hands. A student will train through three stages of schooling philosophy: the handbag on the table, the heavy hanging bag and the person-to-person sensitivity techniques. All three are practiced at the same time. One teaches to condition the hand; another to penetrate the power and energy into a heavy vertical mass; and yet another involves working with a partner, which is done with protective body gear and simulates a real physical encounter. This is truly the most crucial and dangerous part of training; a mistake can result in temporary or permanent injury to the practitioner. A student develops a certain amount of confidence once he sees the potency of the strikes.

Table Bag Training

Hours of training are spent on the table bag. The training bag is filled with sand, stones or iron pellets, and a student will begin with the sand for several months. He will then move to the stone training. They may stay at this level of training for a few years, then they will spend several years conditioning and developing the technique needed to penetrate the iron pellets. This type of training will help develop the bones, skin, tendons, ligaments and muscle.

Ideally, the bag will be made of canvas material and filled with the required substance. It should be about 16 inches in diameter, and placed on a strong wooden table that is about mid-thigh in elevation. These requirements are important for the success of the student's training. The practitioner should maintain a high horse-riding stance during his workout.

In the beginning, training on the table bag is done once a day, three times a week. After a few months, a student will move to twice a day, three times a week, followed eventually by practice three times a day. A Pai Lum Tao student starts off with six basic strikes done on the table bag with sand for approximately six months, followed by stone for approximately six months. Then the student will strike the table bag filled with iron pellets for the duration of his training. The average time of true proficiency in his table bag training is approximately two-and-a-half to three-and-a-half years.

Table bag training is truly the "conditioning" aspect of the iron hand training, and must be cautiously pursued. Serious injury may occur if a student deviates from the proven formulas of his training. Patience and respect for this ancient training is a must.

While traveling the pounding road, the student will condition his hands to penetrate, crush and destroy anything in the attacker's arsenal. Those who have never traveled this road of knowledge can only imagine its awesome power. So much power is developed that intermediate and advanced students must always be cognizant of safety precautions. The damage done with this training can be extremely harmful or lethal to the receiver.

Heavy Bag Training

While a student practices his conditioning, he will also make time to train in the heavy bag training theories. The student will practice executing the strikes to a larger, solid mass target. This allows a chance to attain a more realistic understanding of this remarkable training.

The anxious student will practice striking into the heavy bag with as much power as possible. These practice routines utilize the basic six strikes of iron hand training. The body begins to resemble a whip, with the waist preceding the strike into the bag. Nothing is held back during this phase of training. With every strike comes a balance of power, movement, breathing and expelling.

The matching footwork is the routines of the dragon and monkey. All foot pattern series are practiced in harmony with the punching routines. After several thousands routines, there will become a marriage of motion. This motion will give the student the maximum in power and penetration.

These patterns are known as the cutting, stomping, dotting and the slapping. Each pattern is unique. The student may become more proficient in one technique over another. Particular attention is put into the training to be sure that each pattern is equal if possible.

PERSON-TO-PERSON TRAINING

The final discipline of external iron hand training is the person-to-person routines, which are practiced to understand the realism and effects with a partner. This type of training in the Pai Lum Tao system is known as Dim Hsueh, which alludes to the pinpoint targetry and accuracy of the lethal iron hand strikes.

Dim Hsueh is considered to be among the most advanced training exercises in the Chinese martial arts. All parts of the practitioner's hand are utilized for striking. The strikes theoretically would disrupt the nervous system, interfere with the cardiovascular flow through the vessels, create internal bruising and ultimately render the attacker helpless. The skillful students will practice their timing, speed and accuracy during these sparring practices. Once again, great emphasis is put on safety and care for partners.

The six basic strikes of Pai Lum Tao's iron hand training are used to strike to the 15 basic target points.

These points are:

Crown of the head

Throat

Sternum

Solar plexus

Back of the head

Behind the ear

Seventh vertebrae in upper back

Naval

The groin

Kidneys

Arm pit

Collarbone

Between the biceps and triceps

The wrist

Top of the hand

INTERNAL TRAINING

Internal iron hand drills usually consist of healing and curative exercises, often intended to balance the potential negative effects of the pounding external training. Students also practice the various standing meditations, breathing patterns and visual concentration exercises found within Quan Yen Chi Kung and Chin Kon Pai meditation. If a student does not practice the breathing movements, meditate and fails to apply dit da jow to the proper areas at the proper time, there will be an non-constructive effect on one's health and mental well-being.

Before the Pai Lum Tao student begins any external practice, he will meditate for the necessary time to rid his mind of distractions and negativity. The average time is about 30 minutes. During this time, the breathing exercises are practiced. These routines are known as the practice of Chin Kon Pai within the Pai Lum Tao system. They assist in the chi flow as well as blood flow and distribution required during the coming drills.

With the proper balance of the soft and hard principles the practitioner will be better prepared for his rigorous journey. He will diligently train with the six combination theories.

They are:

Body unifies with the mind

Mind unifies with the thought

Thought unifies with energy

Energy unifies with the spirit

Spirit unifies with the movements

Movement unifies with its surroundings

This internal practice will help unblock the energy meridians throughout the body. It will allow the chi to flow easier and feed energy to the cells in the body. While practicing the routines, one will feel a boost in energy and power that will resemble a powerful wave in the ocean. At the same time, he will remain calm and serene.

The 14 major energy meridians nurtured are:

Conception vessel

Pericardium strait

Gallbladder strait

Heart strait

Lung strait

Large intestine

Small intestine

Governing vessel

Kidney strait

Liver strait

Spleen strait

Triple warmer strait

Stomach strait

Urinary strait

Once the student begins his movement, it is important not to lose his unity of mind, body and spirit. Four basic principles help maintain this natural harmony. These principles must become as natural as taking a breath. They are:

Maintain one's center point

Keep weight distributed properly

Stay completely relaxed

Expel one's chi with proper direction

The unity of internal and external philosophies is achieved by practicing quiet mind, focus, silent movement and natural breathing. These formulas will help the student weather and prevail during their fascinating journey down Pai Lum Tao's pounding road and provide veneration for the crushing iron hand. These techniques and discipline are what separate Bok Leen Pai from so many other Martial Arts systems.

Dr. Daniel Kalimaahaaee was a world-renowned Iron Palm practitioner

Chapter 10
The Five Animals

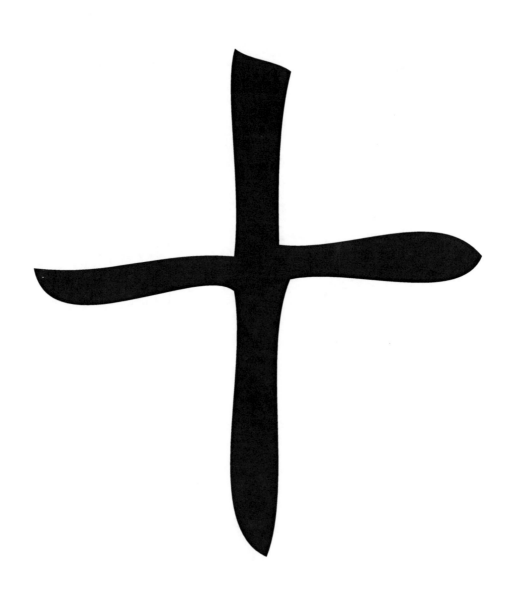

Tiger

The Tiger – Bone / Fire

In the Pai Lum system we understand that the Tiger fears nothing. It is aggressive and powerful, therefore, when hunting its prey, the tiger does not hesitate in any way. Its strong attacks are so powerful it usually maims or kills in a single blow.

The movements of the tiger are usually straight and incorporate deep, rooted stances from which power is generated. The footwork involved with a tiger movement is firm and aggressive. The most common weapon of the tiger is the claw. This claw is used to penetrate and tears across a target.

The movements of the tiger are used to develop the strength of the bone, tendons and ligaments. Isometric/tension type exercises are practiced with regulated breathing to assist in one's health.

As the tiger journeys through the jungle, it fears nothing. It utilizes its renowned courage, prowess, strength and power to overcome all adversaries. These virtues are the very basis of the philosophies and formulas utilized and popularized in the Pai Lum Tao system of martial arts.

Yes, you will find traditional tiger within the white dragon style of martial arts. How can this be? Great Grandmaster Daniel Kane Pai taught his disciples the white dragon can change shape, matter, substance and techniques. So while the diligent practitioner proclaims to be a white dragon, his training will encompass the traditional animals of tiger, crane, leopard, snake, monkey, mantis, white ape and, of course, the ever-powerful white dragon.

Wealth of Knowledge

Each animal is a different discipline of training for the eager student. The different virtues are studied to understand the "mindset" of the techniques to be applied. The ancients passed on a wealth of knowledge from their observations of animals in combative encounters. The Pai Lum Tao practitioner will concentrate on one philosophy at a time to thoroughly understand what the individual animal would think and apply in a specific situation. These individual "animal virtues" will focus on balance, endurance, patience, strength, power, pinpoint targetry, cunningness, and focus. This vast arsenal of "philosophies of execution", which have survived the test of time and been augmented by modern-day influences, is what has made Pai Lum Tao a fiercely respected system in today's topsy-turvy, who's-system-works-and-who's-doesn't world.

When the bright-eyed Pai Lum Tao student enters the fierce world of the tiger he will prepare his training for months of endless conditioning. This conditioning will encompass the strengthening of the sinew and muscle closest to the bone of the arm. Individual finger exercises become as repetitious as breathing during class. Thousands upon thousands of exercises will be done to make the "fu jow" as unyielding as a vice. These various exercises will include finger presses, finger flicks, iron bag, ball squeezing and two-man seven star training. When the student has proven his worthiness by demonstrating a proficient level in these exercises then he is ready to enter the world of the fierce tiger of Pai Lum Tao.

Vast Array of Weapons

The tiger movements found in Pai Lum Tao encompass both short- and long-range movements. This allows the practitioner to choose from the vast array of weapons offered to execute on his opponent. These techniques are executed with blinding speed as well as isometric seizing and controlling with the powerful fu jow tiger claw.

The fu jow is utilized in a varied amount of techniques. These include swiping, clamping, tearing, jabbing and punching. The swiping is a lightning-fast rake across a mass target area. The victim is cut apart before he realizes the swiping claw has been executed. Clamping claws lock on the flesh,joints, tendons and pressure points. Once the clamp has been made the Pai Lum practitioner seizes and controls the attacker with tremendous and unyielding strength. Once the pierce has been made the tiger then tears through the flesh, removing everything in its path. Jabbing techniques are done in blinding speed to vital, softer target areas. The claw will penetrate, stunning the nervous system, and recoil with lightning speed. This will leave the opponent stunned long enough for the finish-up techniques.

The punching routines are done by the tiger closing the paw into an iron hard weapon used for pounding and crushing. Many routines will utilize pounding techniques to soften up the attackers and set the stage for the "seizing claw" to seal the opponent's inevitable fate.

These fierce techniques are visible in the array of traditional tiger forms found in Pai Lum Tao such as Short Form Of The Tiger, Movements Of The Tiger, Twisting Tiger, Tiger Goes Hunting, Outer Tiger and Inner Tiger. Through these prearranged combative routines, the student masters the very essence of the tiger

Five-Element Power

As in all of Pai Lum Tao's teachings the tiger virtues are enhanced by the development of one's chi. This is done through the five elements applications. These elements are air, water, wood, metal and fire. These teachings for development and mastery of chi blended with the animal virtues truly adds credence to the genius of the teaching of Great Grandmaster—Daniel Kane Pai.

The white dragon's moves are classically performed with smooth rhythmic motion that utilizes maximum power and speed. Striking techniques are executed with rapid-fire repetition to an array of target areas.

If there is one thing that history has shown us, it is that Pai Lum works. For as Grandmaster Pai was heard to say many times, "If it doesn't work, it isn't Pai Lum."

To enhance all the physical techniques, proper breathing is greatly stressed to the practitioner. The regulating breath of chi kung is taught to the student, while matching the physical motion with the internal flow of energy is greatly stressed. The movements of the strike must be in total balance with the air flow. There must be a "marriage of motion", just as in the principles of yin and yang.

This harmony of training will surely increase a student's abilities and performance, for as in all Pai Lum Tao techniques, the "tiger virtues" of movement must be all powerful with stunning results. As the tiger travels through time it will fear no attack. It will take the path to avoid confrontation, but when the encounter is inevitable, Pai Lum's fierce tiger virtues will prevail.

The Ever-Changing Dragon
The Dragon – Spirit / Water

The dragon was a symbolic guardian and was the source of true wisdom. The Chinese dragon was a long, slender creature, revered as being wise, and was capable of great feats of illusion and power. A dragon could appear and disappear and change form at will. "The Dragon reveals himself only to vanish." Shaolin monks saw him as a vision of enlightened truth to be felt, but never to be held.

At times the old masters were referred to as dragons, being well versed in the both the healing arts, and kung fu. These skills were a matter of life or death, and those who had mastered them were held in high esteem. They were the masters.

In Pai Lum Tao, the movements based on the dragon incorporate stretching and twisting movements with intricate foot work. Dragon movements often begin with soft circular movements, and end with a hard, sudden explosion of power. The waist is also used to generate power in these movements. This demonstrates the whipping action of the dragon's tail.

These movements are used to build the spirit when used in conjunction with proper breathing. The movements should be executed with relaxed, low breathing until the culmination of the strike, at which point, a sudden exhale will assist in the transmission of power.

No animal within the Asian culture is as revered as the dragon. The very mention of the dragon creates thoughts of "all knowledge," "continuous change," or "spiritual development" — in essence, the highest level of one's self-achievement. Found deep in the cultural teachings of the dragon lies a family system of health, wellness and martial arts. It has come to be known as "lung pai" or "white dragon."

At the center of the philosophy and execution of theories lies the way of the white dragon, better known as Pai Lum Tao. This esoteric style has set a standard of learning and sharing within martial and cultural circles. The way of the white dragon is a strong belief in one's power, speed, and technique.

Changing Shapes

A virtue taught within the dragon animal style is that, "The dragon change shape and form at will." It is believed that if a dragon must become more powerful, he changes into a tiger or white ape. If the situation requires more agility and speed, the crane, monkey or mantis would suffice. However, few wide-eyed beginners will meet the standards needed to be accepted into the "golden ring of learning," which signifies achieving a level of knowledge in Pai Lum Tao. The "rings of learning" are required levels of achievement, attained status, and ranking in the traditional Pai Lum Tao style as authorized by the late Grandmaster, Dr. Daniel Kane Pai.

Pai Lum Tao has nine rings of learning within the study of animal combative virtues: dragon, tiger, crane, snake, leopard, white ape, monkey, praying mantis, and shark.

Stances

Dragon stances incorporate circular evasive stepping patterns, which confuse and unbalance the opponent. These constant changes in the stepping routines challenge   an opponent to constantly catch up to, and not be overcome by, the body.

Using circular footwork, you interlace the figure-8 patterns, linear short lines and ghost walking patterns. The goal of any practitioner is to set and maintain "rhythm of motion." The knowledge to choose the correct pattern at the precise time comes through thousands of test runs practiced over many years. This discipline is divided into two major teachings of stance work: stationary stance and transitionary stance.

Stationary stance work comes into play when establishing a foundation for a block or strike. Low, powerful stances are practiced daily to develop power and stability in the legs. Pai Lum Tao practitioners who make it to the "dragon" level of inner training will develop legs of iron. When a student performs something as simple as a leg sweep, his opponent feels as if an iron bar has struck him. These results require time and discipline "on the floor," which is a common term heard in Pai Lum Tao kwoons (schools).

Whipping Action

Transitionary stance work, which comes into play when a practitioner is most vulnerable to attack, is commonly executed more quickly than the stationary theories of stance. These movements are light, quick, agile, and well timed while coordinated in a distinct rhythm of motion. The energy starts in the "root" or "stance" within dragon philosophy.

It then moves upward into the posture or body dragon training. As energy moves up through the practitioner's legs, the power created is regenerated in the waist whipping action. This particular training is found in the body/posture theories.

Whipping from the waist greatly magnifies the intensity, power and penetration of the strike. When blended with proper stance, the motion will not give the strike away.

Dragon theory often employs the footwork of the monkey while executing a transitionary stance. Because of the many circular, evasive moves of dragon, blending the light, ever-changing patterns of monkey creates a magical symphony of movement. The attacker finds himself lost while attempting to read the dragon's movements. When the time is right the dragon practitioner executes a blinding barrage of counterstrikes.

Armed with an ever-changing series of foot patterns, the Pai Lum Tao student will have an array of versatile counters at his disposal. By simply altering the stance or footwork, a single punch or strike can be delivered from a multitude of angles.

Stances:

1. Square

2. Twisting Horse

3. Bow & Arrow

4. Monkey Step

5. Side Horse

6. Rising Horse

Strikes

Proper breathing should accompany the rhythms of the body. A short breath would be executed with a short-range technique, while a long breath would be followed by a long-range technique. A poison snake "hissing sound" would be utilized with a chin na or dim hsueh technique.

"Poison hand" techniques are taught only in the advanced curriculum. The eager Pai Lum Tao student looks forward to being accepted into this elite training.

The first aspect of poison hand training will encompass the distribution and manipulation of chi. Next comes the fascinating teachings of the three negative points of the hand working in harmony with the three positive points of the foot. Knowledge of vital striking points is at the heart of white dragon martial arts' advanced teachings. Late Great Grandmaster Dr. Daniel Kane Pai was revered for his mastery of the pin chuh theories of the Hopei Region. He passed on this knowledge to only a few chosen disciples.

Understanding the organization and function of one's body and that of his opponent's are keys to mastering Pai Lum Tao's striking theories. With this understanding, punches and kicks move in harmony with chi flow and lead to an explosion at the time of point penetration.

Short and Explosive

The key to dragon techniques can be found primarily in the southern school of teaching. The strikes, for the most part, are short range and explosive, with the technique delivered into the target as opposed to the surface. The technique does not stop at the target; rather, it cuts through the target. Great caution must be practiced when executing these techniques, because improper penetration can lead to serious injury.

Pai Lum Tao's dragon arsenal employs both "gong" hard hand and "yuen" soft hand strikes. The hands will follow the figure-eight linear or circular path. These crushing, slicing, clawing or piercing strikes will be executed quickly — often many times a second — to overwhelm an opponent.

The body should remain relaxed, yet firm when strikes are executed. Tight muscles or joints restrict energy flow and interfere with sinew and muscle movement, which is vital for the proper execution of the technique.

The explosive movements of the dragon can be devastating. The strikes penetrate a few inches into the target with a linear motion, and then cut through with a circular motion.

Some commonly used "dragon hands" are:

- Ram's Head Punch

- Dragon's Head

- Twin Dragons Searching for the Pearl

- Eye of the Phoenix

- Twin Dragon's Head

- Pecking Bird

- Immortal Man Points the Way

- Hook Punch

- Uppercut

- Five Star

- Dragon's Claw

- Spear Finger

- Dragon's Breath

These disciplined strikes will be practiced using the theories found in the "short breath" and "long breath" techniques and will be mastered through Quan Nien Chi Kung exercises. Taught from day one in traditional Pai Lum Tao training, these essential breathing patterns require many years of diligent study to master the unification of inner and outer wu kung.

Maximum Penetration

The formulas and theories of execution behind Pai Lum Tao's kicks vary little from those of the hand strikes. Originally, white dragon stylists never kicked above waist. Today, however, its not uncommon to see practitioners kicking to the head or performing elegant jump kicks. All kicks are delivered with relaxation and fluid motion to allow for maximum penetration. Rooting the supporting leg provides a fulcrum effect, which allows the rest of the body to swing and rotate and ensures good balance is maintained throughout the technique.

Kicks must be angled to guarantee positive results. If a stylist wants to dislodge an attacker's balance he may have to drive up his kick. The practitioner might begin with a linear kick to dislodge his opponent's balance. He would then rotate his body and drop his stability level. Finally, if he wants to cause extreme injury, he takes down the attacker and delivers a kick in a downward direction. The attack will have no answer for this penetrating kick; his body will buckle from the explosion and hit the ground hard.

Pai Lum Tao kicks found in the dragon key training include:

- Wheel
- Roundhouse
- Dragon Spins Tail
- Inside Crescent Moon
- Outside Crescent Moon
- Knife Edge
- Stomp
- Chopping Ax
- Scooping Spade
- Knee Strikes
- Front Snap

Dragon theories, like their footwork and animal virtue, are ever changing. It is this adaptability to the situation, to the opponent, which separates its movements from those found in other styles. Lightning speed, total relaxation with enhanced chi flow, maximum power at the time of penetration; this is the essence of Pai Lum Tao's dragon virtues.

The Evasive White Crane
The Crane - Balance / Metal

The crane is the most graceful and patient of the animals found in Pai Lum Tao. It is often seen standing on one leg deep in thought. When confronted, the crane does not attack straight on, but instead uses its legs and wings to evade away from its adversary, striking when an opening occurs. The crane will utilize both its beak and its wings to fight. Although the crane is usually smaller and more frail than it's opponent, it can be a ferocious adversary. It is very mobile, this allows it to move where it cannot be attacked, but can attack easily. The crane's beak is pointed, allowing it to strike to a smaller target area; usually vital areas of the body are targeted. The crane's beak can also be used as a blocking technique when used with a long, circular motion of the arms.

In Pai Lum Tao the movements of the crane are used to train inner harmony and balance. One way to do this is the crane stance, where one stands with one leg firmly rooted into the ground and the opposite knee is lifted up vertically, so that the practitioner could balance a tea cup on their knee.

The Key To Success

Understanding the depth and zones of attack are keys to the combative success of Pai Lum Tao. Depth of short- and long-hand boxing become the basic categories of study within the system. To know which strategy to use and when becomes the science of the warrior.

The devastating long hand techniques of Pai Lum Tao teach one to strike like a whip. The body is kept relaxed and supple while the hand emulates a metal ball. This allows the practitioner to move in the "nei," soft and smooth, and strike in the "wei," hard and powerful. Maximum range is the goal of the "long wing" movements. The muscle, tendons and sinew are worked continuously to assure their flexibility at the time of execution. Exercises such as swing arm, horizontal whips and extended wings are practiced daily. Arms become extremely strong yet supple; this ensures good "chi" flow when the technique reaches its destination. The short hand techniques slice, pierce and crush in circular, vertical, horizontal and figure eight patterns. These moves are kept close to the body and require countless hours of speed drills to assure the "lightning-fast" snapping motion. Such drills as pecking beak, crane's head and spearing the enemy assure pinpoint targetry. These drills are practiced solo for speed and technique and with a partner for timing and targetry. They move quickly in close range and are accentuated by powerful waist whipping. The attacker who runs into the short-range combative techniques will quickly fall or yield back into the long-range zones.

Encompassing both long hand and short hand, a variety of hand and arm arsenals are practiced diligently. Basic hand strikes such as spear, leopard, sun, ram, uppercut, backfist, heel palm, willow palm, crane's beak and crane's head are the essential utensils. The arm is used to open up or crush anything in its path. Arm strikes begin with white cranes wing, white ape, on-guard, searching rod, and bear. These techniques serve as a battering ram to offset, dislodge and disrupt the attacker's flow.

Back To Basics

Before the Pai Lum Tao practitioner can hope to master his arsenal he will spend countless hours working the basic disciplines of stance, posture, and technique. Then he must understand the principles of distance and depth. This will determine the warrior's "plan of action" - which technique to use with the long-hand sets and which to use with the short-hand series.

Once the mind has sent the signal, the techniques must be reactionary. With this reactionary response Pai Lum Tao's white crane theories evolve around a speedy, powerful execution of technique. This is a formula that cannot be successful without the ingredients of both lightning and thunder; speed techniques must be simultaneous in nature. One may not have the luxury of time to think of a response to an attack. Speed drills must be practiced on a daily basis. The key to speed is relaxation. The pupil is taught to move in the "nei" soft-smooth movements. Such exercises as picking the fruit, thunder and lightning and elusive wind are practiced diligently to insure that one develops and maintains the lightning speed for which Pai Lum Tao has become known.

Power must be built from the ground up. Stance is the root of the movement. A weak stance may prove disastrous for the practitioner. The three-step formula of "stance, posture, then technique" becomes a "checkpoint" for the student to gauge his success in preparation. The student is trained to understand the full effectiveness of "waist whipping" of the dragon. The waist whipping can triple the power of a punch when executed correctly. With a smooth, fluid motion the waist will precede the punch then recoil to its "set" position. With this immense power the punch will then be able to penetrate with a magnified result.

Physical and mental training play a most important role in the success of the outcome of a conflict. Physical training can be complex and dangerous if not instructed by the proper tutor. Iron body training is part of the practitioner's carefully practiced formula. The conditioning of the body to not feel pain when the punch or kick lands is a slow, careful process. Thousands of carefully placed strikes by a trained partner will become routine. Herbal medicine, such as dragon dit da jow, will be essential for protection of external and internal bruises that may occur during rigorous training. With this in mind, partner training such as "seven star" becomes common place.

Finding The Perfect Balance

Balance is just as important as speed and power. The very essence of white crane training evolves around balance. Balance encompasses stance, posture, technique, execution, timing and breathing.

Balance training begins with the cat stance (low and high) and works toward the sleeping crane — on one leg for 15 minutes. This is slow, yet direct training designed to reach the level desired by the students. Mastery of balance is key for any student who wants to become proficient in his art.

Pinpoint striking is a well-known characteristic of the white crane. Knowing where to strike can make the difference between success and failure. The technique will be partially determined by the practitioner based on his target area. Pai Lum Tao's white crane teaches fingers to pierce; blade of hand to slice: palm of hand to stun; and fist hand to crush.

They say that "timing is everything." But as most martial artists know, perfecting "timing" is one of the most difficult training aspects to conquer. Students will practice a cat-and-mouse type of training with a partner. The offensive partner attempts to tag his defensive partner's extended palms with a variety of crane strikes while the palms are moving. The moving palms will be purposely deceptive and evasive to the attack. This teaches one to relax and explode spontaneously with pinpoint accuracy.

Off Balance And Confused

The crane teaches us the epitome of patience. While practicing white crane, a student practices patience as he moves about the floor in a smooth, fluid motion. Once his opponent obligates himself, and ultimately compromises his guard, the white crane explodes with a beautiful flurry of techniques which render the attacker helpless. Such development in one's patience is a time-tested discipline which separates the winners and losers.

The ever-changing movements of white crane keep its attacker off balance and confused. There is a continuous linking of movements in a systematic array of strikes. The Pai Lum Tao practitioner's goal is to develop spontaneous reaction. Movements link into one another with a rhythm of energy release. One will not only begin to read his attacker's moves, but he will actually predetermine them by his own movement.

Pai Lum Tao puts a great emphasis on the combined development of mind, body, and spirit. The practitioner learns that the mind triggers the body, the body awakens the spirit, and the spirit creates the mind.

The natural blending of the three creates a true harmony. This is never more evident than in Pai Lum Tao's white crane.

STRIKES	KICKS	STANCES
Ram's Head	Front Heel	Square Horse
Hooking Hand	Stomp	Side Horse
Willow Palm	Side Heel	Cat
Crane's Beak	Monk's Spade	Single Leg
Crane's Head	Front Broom	Long Bow
Lifting Hand	Back Broom	Short Bow
Outside Wing	Inside Crescent	Twisting Horse
Inside Wing	Outside Crescent	Hidden Stance
Uppercut	Tornado	
Noni Slap	Back	
Crane Grab	Knife Edge	
Backfist		

Explosive Leopard

The Leopard – Muscle / Wood

Although a powerful animal, the leopard does not have the size or mass of say, a tiger or ape. Thus, it cannot use just brute strength in a combative situation. Instead, the leopard relies on its efficiency of its muscle and movements coupled with speed. When the leopard pounces on its victim, it will apply a series of fast and unrelenting techniques.

The fast strikes of the leopard are executed using quick footwork and speedy hands. Because of their quick nature, the movements of the leopard do not emphasize blocking. The leopard would use a slight shift to evade followed immediately by a series of fast angular attacks. The most common leopard technique is a claw, but unlike the tiger which is both crushing and tearing, the leopard will rake the target.

The movements of the leopard are used to develop muscle efficiency, not to build up muscle. This develops both power and speed. Leopard training will develop discipline and develop ones patience. The lower body will become extremely strong and enhance the ability to spring powerfully into the air.

As in most styles of ancient fighting the leopard style was established through the observation of the movements of the leopard in the wild, therefore practitioners of Bok Leen Pai Kenpo will imitate the various movements. The philosophy of hit and run techniques of the leopard are especially effective against larger, slower and more stationary opponents.

The primary weapon is the leopard fist, claw and various palm strikes. Other weapons utilized are the Ram's Head punch, Reverse Ram's Head punch, Eye Of The Phoenix and the Sun Fist. Power striking, clawing and grabbing as well as pin point puncturing are all theories used by the Leopard practitioner.

One of the fascinating attributes of Leopard is the ability to simultaneously block and strike the opponent. This creates a powerful explosion of technique. Though this is commonly practiced in all the disciplines of Pai Lum Tao Martial Arts it is most showcased in the powerful Leopard techniques. The Leopards sheer speed, power, agility, cunningness and athletic abilities set it apart from many styles.

Rhythmic Snake
The Snake – Chi / Earth

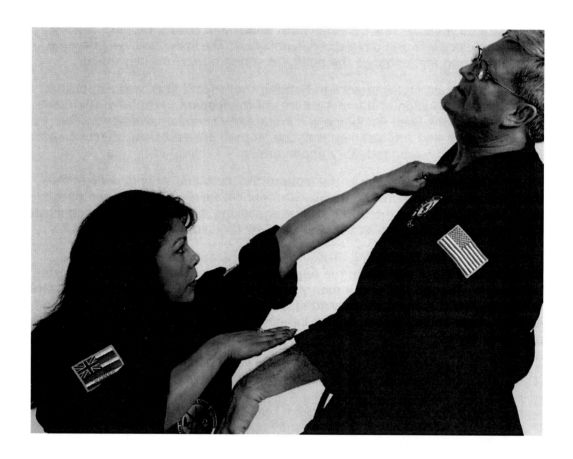

The snake has no legs or arms, requiring it to move using a circular motion of its body. When threatened, the snake is a vicious opponent. The snake strikes with speed and accuracy to vital areas such as pressure points and soft targets. The power of a snake's strike comes from the speed and momentum of its coiled body. It is known for its cunning and soft nature.

To maximize effectiveness, the movements of the snake are executed in long stretched stances; this allows more leverage during striking. The fingertips are used as the main weapon of the snake and are used to penetrate vital areas of the opponent.

Utilizing several breathing exercises coupled with their soft and flowing nature, the movements of the snake are used to develop Chi. These soft, flowing movements will bring the practitioner to a relaxed and peaceful state, allowing them to develop their Chi to a higher level.

Practitioners of snake style martial arts claim that performing the fluid movements of snakes allows them to entwine with their opponent's attack as defense and strike them from multiple angles. You would see this in the sticking hands training. This type of training is popular in southern styles. The smooth, sensitive and fluid movements of the snake are very practical in theory and are the basis to many soft style martial arts.

Bok Leen Pai maintains two separate philosophies of application. One imitates the Cobra with pin point striking to vulnerable areas and teaches the theories of venom striking. The other imitates the Python by wrapping around and constricting movement of the opponent, eventually suffocating them. When taught properly both of these philosophies of motion and execution will work with great harmony and effectiveness.

It is most commonly believed that our snake style martial arts were developed at and near the Southern Shaolin Temple in Fukien Province which was sometimes called the snake temple. Bok Leen Pai snake also has it's roots in the 5 Animal, Hung and Choy families of Chuan Fa in China. The snake movements are based upon their whipping power which is generated in the waist and travels up the spine to the fingers. At that point 'Chi' is transferred out the finger tips and injected into the target. Generally one aims for the weak points of the body such as eyes, throat, groin and joints. Compressing one's stomach/abdominal muscles is very important and essential to maximize the whipping action. Straight punches such as the Ram's head, Hooking fist and Sun fist are the primary power strikes. Butterfly Palms, Willow Palms, Upper Cut, Back Fist, Spear Hand and the White Snake Head (thrusting fingers) techniques are the mainstay of the striking arsenal.

The kicking techniques of Bok Leen Pai Snake are generally down to the middle and lower gates. That is to the target areas are the rib cage, lower back, and all parts of the legs. On occasion it is not uncommon to see a kicking strike to the attacker's arm. The arsenals of kicks are varied. The most common are the Inside And Outside Crescent, these particular whipping kicks fit in nicely with the philosophy of White Snake Combat. Other kicks commonly utilized are the Front

Snap, Knife Edge Side Heel and Back Kick, as varied as typical northern styles with high kicks, but also typical are below-the-knee kicks seen in southern styles. An obvious difference in kicking between the snake and the other animals is that many times the 'big toe' will be utilized as a striking tool.

Since much of the movements and transformation of this style are performed low to the ground, footwork and stance are extremely important. The footing must be well grounded at all times. The stance transition must be flowing in order to maximize the whipping action of any technique. The practitioner must build a strong torso and spine to be able to generate and allow 'Chi' to travel properly through the body and then adequately expel out the fingers.

Of the famous 'Five Animals,' Snake is considered the main style which eventually led to or influenced several internal styles of training. The smooth and fluid motion coupled with the cultivating of Chi made the snake style unique. Within Bok Leen Pai the internal art of Quan Nien Chi Kung is taught to all students regardless of their major discipline. It is, however, never more prevalent or obvious than when a student is practicing the snake style. This internal training helps greatly when a student tries to develop their patience and the synchronization of the harmony of breath and physical motion. The student must pay attention to detail and precision. They must learn the discipline training of repetition and have an understanding of articulate behavior. The snake is patient, clever and utilizes every skill it was born with.

Once a student has progressed in the snake style they will enter the highest level of training - Poison Hand. The Snake practitioner will learn the vital points to strike to and how to strike them. This training is found in a specific Bok Leen Pai training known as Dim Shui. Hitting these areas correctly will cause an attacker to become dizzy, weak, disorientated, unconscious or to die. This high level of training is taught only to the most entrusted and deserving student. The practitioner will spend a lot of time working on their precision, timing and accuracy.

Chapter 11
Fist Sets - Short Battles

Bok Leen Pai Kenpo

Fist Sets – Story Of The Battles

"Fist sets tell the stories of the battles, while Forms tell the stories of the wars."

Through its intricate movements the stories of the system are passed on from generation to generation through the practice of the fist sets. They are short sequences of movements that depict a self defense encounter.

A student will practice these traditional short routines to develop their martial arts skills, confidence and to find a certain peace within. This peace and confidence comes from working one's routines hundreds of times in multiple situations. There is no guarantee as to how an attack may happen and a student must be adaptable to any and all conflicts.

The variation of challenges found at the core of the fist sets is extremely varied and covers all situational attacks. These variables include but are not limited to punches, kicks, grabs, chokes, head locks, joint locks, thrown objects, weapon attacks as well as multiple attackers.

These routines will challenge a practitioner's endurance, power, rhythm, speed, pin point targetry, foresight, self confidence and their total understanding of the Bok Leen Pai Kenpo art. A certain 'air' of one's self will develop with the cultivation of their fist sets. The better they master their fist sets the more their confidence and self reason as a person is defined.

The Hawaiian martial arts are famous for their self defense and combat abilities and Bok Leen Pai Kenpo is no exception. With many decades of modern development and centuries of historical travels from China and Okinawa a practitioner will come to know the honor of learning these stories of battle and triumph. They will understand the warrior's code – "Seek peace always, but if the soul is threatened, let the soul become WARRIOR".

Self Defense Fist Sets
'Stories Of The Short Battles'

1. Riding The Dragon Through Heaven

2. White Ape Grasping The Heavens

3. Retreating Monkey

4. Laughing Monkey

5. Walking Spirit

6. Wandering Black Tiger

7. Crane Dries It's Wings

8. Snake Sheds It's Skin

9. Constricting Serpent

10. Driving Tiger

11. Circling Crane

12. Dance Of Death

13. Falcon's Flight

14. Continuous Thunder

15. Escaping Tiger

16. Striking From Heaven

17. Kick Of The Tiger

18. Pounding Jackal

19. Leopard Palm

20. Tiger And Crane Search

21. Twisting Crane

22. Clinging Serpent

23. Playful Monkey

1. Riding The Dragon Through Heaven

1a

1b

1c

1d

2. White Ape Grasping The Heavens

2a

2b

2c

2d

3. Retreating Monkey

3a

3b

3c

3d

4. Laughing Monkey

4a

4b

4c

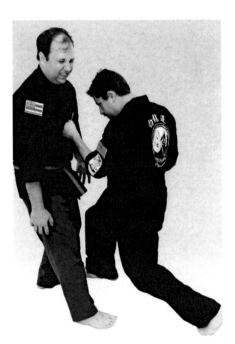

4d

5. Walking Spirit

5a

5b

5c

5d

6. Wandering Black Tiger

6a

6b

6c

6d

7. Crane Dries Its Wings

7a

7b

7c

8. Snake Sheds Its Skin

8a

8b

8c

9. Constricting Serpent

9a

9b

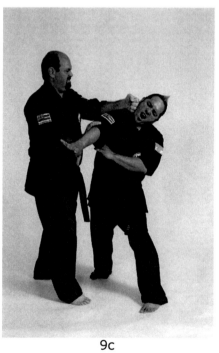

9c

9d

10. Driving Tiger

10a

10b

10c

10d

10e

11. Circling Crane

11a

11b

11c

11d

12. Dance of Death

12a

12b

12c

12d

12e

12f

13. Falcon's Flight

13a

13b

13c

14. Continuous Thunder

14a

14b

14c

15. Escaping Tiger

15a

15b

15c

15d

16. Striking From Heaven

16a

16b

16c

16d

17. Kick of the Tiger

17a kick of the tiger

17b

17c

17d

18. Pounding Jackal

18a pounding jackal

18b

18c

19. Leopard Palm

19a

19b

19c

19d

20. Tiger and Crane Search

20a

20b

20c

20d

20e

21. Twisting Crane

21a

21b

21c

21d

21e

22. Clinging Serpent

22a

22b

22c

22d

23. Playful Monkey

23a

23b

23c

23d

Chapter 12
Form
Tan Tar Pu Shen Su

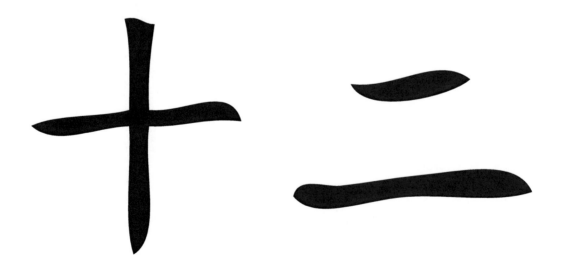

Tan Tar Pu Shen Su

Tan Tar Pu Shen Su – 'Blocking The Line Four' is the fourth form of the six found in this basic series. This form is taught at the very basic level to teach a student how to block their line of defense and crush the attacker's advance then explode with a Reverse Ram's head assault. The form is done low and extremely fast.

The body is kept relaxed and emulates a whip. The strikes - whether blocking or countering - are done fast and with explosive chi into the target area. The idea of breaking anything that enters into one's zone is a standard of Pai Lum Tao – Bok Leen Pai Kenpo teachings.

The breathing is done in short rhythms and must match the physical movement of the practitioner. A student is taught that their energy 'Chi' begins in the root, travels upwards and is regenerated in the whipping of the waist. It is then expelled out the technique and enters the attacker's body at the point of contact of the method used to counter.

A certain rhythm of motion is matched with the attitude of the practitioner. This merging becomes a beautiful artistic expression of the student. They know that the story they are telling is the one of a Dragon Warrior in war. No words are needed, just watch the story played out in front of you. Forms are the backbone of a system and keep it's history intact for generations to come.

1 - Right Inward Parry Hand

2 - Left Upward Block

3 - Right Reverse Ram's Head
Punch

4 - Right Upward Block

5 - Left Reverse Ram's Head
Punch

6 - Set For Downward Block Series

7 - Left Downward Block

8 - Right Reverse Ram's Head
Punch

9 - Right Downward Block

10 - Left Reverse Ram's Head
Punch

11 - Set For Outward Block Series

12 - Left Outward Block

13 - Right Reverse Ram's Head
Punch

14 - Right Outward Block

15 - Left Reverse Ram's Head
Punch

16 - Set For Inward Block Series

17 - Left Inward Block

18 - Right Reverse Ram's Head
Punch

19 - Set With Extended Crane's
Wings for Second Inward Block

20 - Right Inward Block

21 - Left Reverse Ram's Head
Punch

22 - Square Horse Stance

23 - Downward Cross Wing Block
With Gong Chuan

24 - Display Earth Element
Symbol

25 - End in Square Horse Stance

Chapter 13
Nine Sacred Hands

Nine Sacred Hands
Of Bok Leen Pai Kenpo Form

Traditional Salutation

From fist chambered at sides step out with right foot to high square horse.

Stationary Set.

1. Lotus Posture

2. Water Posture

3. Earth Posture

4. Wood Posture

5. Gong Yuen Chuan Posture

6. Snake Hand Posture

7. Spear Hand Posture

8. Ready Stance Posture

9. Neutral stance Posture

Side Horse Set: Right Technique Footwork

Left foot moves to right foot then moves back into side horse stance except it is a little more to the left of a typical side horse. As you lock into stance turn your torso half way back to the starting position (a traditional Kenpo posture) after the technique is executed bring your back foot up to your front foot moving through this position and back to the high square horse stance. Change your hand position and repeat footwork. This applies to all positions except #8. As you bring your back foot up after completing the element for #7. Turn your palms down and recross your arms as your feet come together. Leave them there as you move your foot out into high square horse. Roll over palms and pull fist back to chamber at sides as feet come together to set back into side horse.

Differences in the hand positions from stationary to side horse set:

Wood is extended out roughly one foot in front of the chest while moving into side horse.

Cross over arms palms up and palms down - as you move into side horse the palm away from the attacker moves into chamber position at your side (left palm moves to left side) while remaining in palm up or palm down position depending on which one you are working. The palm closest to the attacker stays out as the primary defense.

The entire sequence is as follows:

SALUTATION

STATIONARY SET

RIGHT SET

LEFT SET

STATIONARY SET

SALUTATION

NOTE: From neutral stance at the END of all sequences your arms crossover right over left and roll over then move out into LOTUS position.

1 - White Lotus Posture

2 - Water Posture

3 - Earth Posture

4 - Wood Posture

5 - Gong Yuen Chuan Posture

6 - Snake Hand Posture

7 - Spear Hand Posture

8 - Ready Stance Posture

9 - Neutral Stance Posture

1A - White Lotus Fighting Stance

2A - Water Fighting Stance

3A - Earth Fighting Stance

4A - Wood Fighting Stance

5A - Gong Yuen Chuan Fighting
Stance

6A - Snake Hand Fighting Stance

7A - Spear Hand Fighting Stance

8A - Ready Fighting Stance

9A - Neutral Fighting Stance

Chapter 14
Weapons

Weapons – The Tool Of The Warrior

When the Bok Leen Pai Kenpo student has become proficient with their empty hand movements and patterns they will be eligible for weapons training. This eligibility is also determined by their attitude and discipline. If the anxious student does not show the required level of honor, loyalty and discipline they may be held back from progressing into the fascinating world of Kenpo weapons training.

A student will begin their journey into the world of weaponry by starting off with the wood element, then they will progress into the metal weapon formulas and then they will be offered the knowledge of the combination of wood and metal weapons. This knowledge will be a combination of technical skills as well as psychological philosophy that must be mastered in addition.

The use of weapons to defend oneself would certainly date back to as long as man has been in existence and has met conflict with animal and other men. The first time a tribesman picked up a branch to defend himself or others from imminent danger, the art of weaponry had begun. The refining and expansion of weaponry would certainly develop as man's need and intelligence evolved. The earliest types of weaponry in Asia would not differ from that of any people existing in ancient times. The stick, stone and leather hides would have been the main stay of utensils available at the time. One thing is for sure, weapons existed before the written language and there is no formal account of man's first use and the evolution of primitive weapons.

At the very beginning of a Bok Leen Pai Kenpo students journey down the road of weapons knowledge will be the 'vision lectures.' These lectures will stimulate ones 'stream of thought.' The weapons enthusiast will learn to clear their mind of nagging and hindering thoughts, for they create distraction and can be self harming! During this crucial time insights and strategies will be passed down from teacher to student. This disciplined process has been perfected for centuries in Asian martial arts. It is believed by many martial arts scholars that this type of teaching is needed now more than ever with our modern societies and cultures.

To those outside the traditional arts 'mastering weaponry' has been greatly misunderstood. This typical misunderstanding of weapons is due to modern movies, our modern society's instant gratification mindset as well as the lack of truly qualified weapons masters. The training should be a form of ritualistic combat where the student becomes the absolute best they can with the prayer of never having to execute the deadly techniques on another human.

An apprentice will train continuously on the most basic element or technique for this builds the foundation of their future learning. Once the foundation is secure and strong the teacher will begin to build this beautiful sculpture within the eager student. Training will intensify and become more difficult to execute. With these increased difficulties the weapons enthusiast will become more entrenched and fascinated with the luminous path they are traveling. They will understand the history of the battles and the culture of the people will become more defined. This type of traditional training ensures the respect and reverence due to each of Kenpo's fascinating weapons.

Crescent Moon Lance

This very unique weapon is rarely seen or practiced. It is a southern Chinese weapon that is a distinctive blend of several different weapons. Within its makeup and utilization you will find the single edge saber, the staff augmented with two crescent moon blades.

This weapon can be used for stabbing, slashing, poking, hooking and trapping. The movements are executed close to the body with circular and linear patterns. One will then combine all of the patterns to create a maze of movements that will be virtually impossible to defend against.

It is taught to the advanced student once they have developed a good understanding of the metal and wood theories of weaponry. A slight mistake with this awesome weapon and an injury is certain.

Double Axes

The doubles axes are one of the most powerful weapons in any arsenal. Due to their heavy weight they are usually utilized by a larger, stronger practitioner. The sheer weight of the axes being swung in circular patterns will chop through anything in its path.

This powerful weapon is used to hack, chop, smash and the shine from the broad head of the axe may be the last memory of any would be foe. With its distinctive construction it can also stab with the spear head or hook and trap with the back side.

The practitioner who chooses to train with the double axes will have many hours of arm conditioning ahead of them. One must build a certain amount of arm, shoulder and upper body strength coupled with flexibility to perform the intricate circular patterns. It is truly one weapon that an adversary would not want to get into its perilous path.

Iron Rings

This distinctive training tool doubles as a weapon. The Chinese have used iron rings for strength and discipline training for centuries. Most practitioners only know its use for training; few know the secrets of its practical use as a hidden weapon.

Iron rings can be worn on the wrist and hidden in the sleeve of a coat. It can then be easily pulled out and grasped by the hand creating an iron fist. The practitioner will strike with it in a hammer fist, ridge hand or slapping motion. These assaults will surprise and confuse the attacker and will obviously do a great deal of damage to any striking surface. The result will often result in the opponent being badly bruised or even having their bones broken.

The Iron rings are another of the rare weapons that are utilized in the Pai Lum Tao system of Martial Arts and another example of why this style is so unique.

Ring Knives

The Ring Knives are another southern Chinese weapon that dates back centuries and is very popular with traditionalists. They are light and very maneuverable. The ring knives can be concealed rather easily and be drawn in preparation for battle instantly.

They are a two sided knife so they are perfect for any slashing motion and when the ring at the end of the handle is used they can spin 360 degrees. A few of the movements that can be utilized are cutting, stabbing, hooking and parrying an attack. A practitioner has the option of tying a scarf on the end of the ring to disguise the movements as well as confuse an opponent.

With such light weight this weapon is popular with women as well as men. Typically the movements will be continuous and will build speed and power with circular motions resulting in a tremendous centrifugal force. Upon observing a routine a person may see a fusion of several techniques executed at lightning speed. These routines become overwhelming to the person who initially attacked the Bok Leen Pai practitioner!

Staff

The staff is the first weapon that the eager Bok Leen Pai student will train in. The lessons learned while working the many exercises of staff are coordination, accuracy, power, speed, endurance and pride in one's tradition. Yes, pride in the fact that now the student will be entering a whole new area of training and discipline. One will learn the history of the weapon and memorize traditional lectures on protocol, respect and how to practice their new found 'warrior spirit'. For now they will utilize a weapon and learn to respect its abilities and teachings.

The staff can be made of rattan, bamboo, white wood or red wood. The traditional staff in Kenpo is always an element of nature and at one time was alive. Its length can very from 4 foot, 6 foot or 8 foot in length. The size of the practitioner may dictate which length they choose to use, but there are distinct movement and formulas of execution for each individual staff size. Therefore, a six foot man may learn the different executions of technique of three different weapons.

Some of the various techniques utilized with the staff are slapping, poking, raking, hooking, full 360 degrees spins and shoving with the center section. When the staff builds up speed and power it makes a distinctive whirling noise very similar to a wind storm. This means that it is generating speed and power and when this comes in contact with the intended target it can be devastating!

Kenpo Two Handed Sword

In Bok Leen Pai Kenpo the patient and disciplined student, after showing his skill with a wooden weapon (staff) will be introduced to the metal weapon (sword). In this case the two handed sword or Katana. The Katana is a curved, single edged Japanese sword and is often mistakenly called the Samurai sword. Samurai is the warrior not the sword. The Katana gets its curve in the way it is cooled or quenched in the process of making it. Prior to quenching it is straight like similar Chinese swords. As a matter of fact, the oldest swords on record in Japan were imported from China to Japan as a present to the Queen in 240 a.d. (Wei-dynasty). Many more were imported in 280 a.d.

In Bok Leen Pai Kenpo the katana is used mainly because they are easy to find and are fairly inexpensive for a good quality product. We respect the sword as a tool that can cut human flesh. Therefore, we clear the mind by acknowledging that the reason we remove the sword from the saya (scabbard) is solely for training. In addition to basic movements of the sword we also practice the beautiful movements of the Seven Ways Of Cutting series and Battle Set, to name a few. The student is also required to know the names of some of the parts of the katana and how to handle it before ever removing it from the scabbard (saya). Safety and maintenance are held in the highest priority. The Bok Leen Pai Kenpo sword forms are as beautiful as they are deadly. The new student will see a series of movements linked together to tell an awesome story of an ancient battle. The trained martial artist will see that each individual cut will take years to master.

When watching these stories unfold, it is clear that there is a balance of Chinese and Japanese influence in the techniques. The ancestry and teachings are clearly that of the Chinese two handed sword which history teaches was the predecessor to the katana of Japan. These Chinese moves blend eloquently with the Japanese katana theories to create a defined 'Pai' version of mastering the sword.

The modern day patterns of 'sword play' in Bok Leen Pai Kenpo were mastered by SiTaiGung Wilson who learned them directly from Great Grandmaster – Dr. Daniel Kalimaahaae Pai in the mid 1970s.

Chapter 15
Salutations

Salutations

The salutation is the signature of the system or style. There are several different signatures that are expressed for various occasions. Two of the most commonly practiced in Bok Leen Pai Kenpo are the Square Horse and the Formal Salutations. They have their similarities and their differences. A distinct message is sent with all salutations and it precedes the communication and closes it out.

Square Horse Salutation

The square horse salutation is the first one that a student will learn. It is the salutation of the warrior standing their ground. The movements are powerful and quick. When the warrior is in battle this salutation means that no one and nothing gets past them.

Ready Stance

Rising Horse Stance

Square Horse Stance

Present Gong Chuan

Cover with Yuen Chuan

Bow Presenting Gong – Yuen Chuan Hands

Clear Zone with Double Gong Chuan

Ready Stance

Draw Chi Up from the Root Chakra

Push Chi Back to the Root Chakra

Square Horse Salutation

1 - Ready Stance

2 - Rising Horse Stance

3 - Square Horse Stance

4 - Present Gong Chuan

5 - Cover with Yuen Chuan

6 - Bow presenting Gong-Yuen Chuan Hands

7 - Clear zone with double Gong Chuan Strikes

8 - Ready Stance

9 - Draw Chi up from the root
Chakra

10 - Push Chi back to the root
Chakra

Formal Salutation

The Formal Salutation is the next one that a practitioner learns and is that of a higher level. This salutation represents ceremonial curriculum and shows that the student has paid their dues on the floor. It is representative of classical Chinese movements and is accurately a signature of the Shaolin heritage that Bok Leen Pai Kenpo possesses.

Break Stance

Draw Gong Yuen Chuan hands back to the left

Clear zone with Gong Yuen hands

Strike with Gong Yuen hands

Grab opponent with hands

Roll Gong Chuan hands over and strike

Ready Stance

Draw Chi up from the Root Chakra

Push Chi back to the Root Chakra

Formal Salutation

1 - Break Stance

2 - Draw Gong Yuen Hands Back
to the Left

3 - Clear Zone With Gong Yuen
Hands

4 - Strike With Gong Yuen
Hands

5 - Grab Opponent With Hands

6 - Roll Gong Chuan Hands Over
and Strike

7 - Ready Stance

8 - Draw Chi Up From the Root
Chakra

9 - Push Chi Back to the Root
Chakra

Chapter 16
Gallery

Dr. Pai with his student & champion Glenn Wilson 1978

Daniel K. Pai, Jay T. Will, Muhammed
Ali

Dr. Daniel K. Pai 1991

Dr. Daniel K. Pai breaks 1000
pounds of ice with palm strike
- famous photo

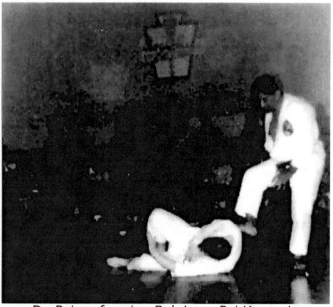

Dr. Pai performing Bok Leen Pai Kenpo in
tournament mid 1960s, very rare photo

Dr. Daniel K. Pai mid 1960s

Dr. Daniel Kalimaahaae Pai -
break stance

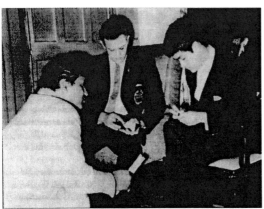

Dr. Daniel Pai, George Dillman and
Bruce Lee exchange business cards
1967

Dr. Daniel Kane Pai and Bruce Lee

Dr. Pai teaching Professor Glenn
Wilson (1)

Dr. Pai teaching Professor Glenn
Wilson (2)

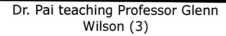

Dr. Pai teaching Professor Glenn
Wilson (3)

Dr. Pai teaching Professor Glenn Wilson (4)

Glenn C. Wilson and Dr. Daniel
Kalimaahaae Pai 1991

Glenn C. Wilson and Paul Yamaguchi

Glenn C. Wilson and Jerry
Pennington

Glenn C. Wilson and Jeff Speakman 1991

Glenn Wilson - Kenpo 1971

Glenn Wilson wins Florida
Classic point fighting 1977

Glenn Wilson and Mike
Perez finalist in Florida
Classic 1977

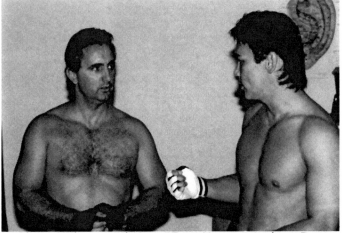

Glenn Wilson and Kung Fu - Kenpo student Don
Wilson 1992

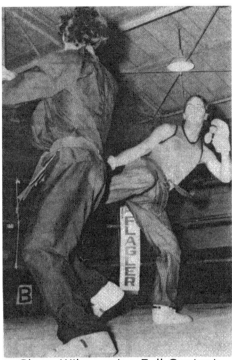

Glenn Wilson wins Full Contact
Match - Florida 1977

Glenn Wilson with Pai Lum students Don
Wilson and Cynthia Rothrock

GM Wilson in Lama Shi Dechou's home
inside Shaolin Temple 2

GM Wilson at Shaolin Temple 2006

Kenpo - Kung Fu U.S. Champions 1977 - Jack Farr, Glenn
Wilson, Eric Lee, Karyn Turner, Peter Morales

Lama De Shou and martial arts brother
Glenn Wilson at the Shaolin Temple

Kenpo pioneer Dr. Daniel K.
Pai 1966

Lama Shi DeChou and Grandmaster Glenn Wilson at Shaolin
Temple China

Pai Lum Tao Security team with champion Don Wilson Las Vegas

Presentation at the Great Wall of China

Professor Yin, Hilda Wilson, Lama De Shou
, Glenn Wilson at Shaolin Temple

Three generations of Pai Lum Tao - Dr. Pai, Prof.
Glenn Wilson, Sifu Don Wilson

Two of Pai Lum Tao's top female Dragon
Warriors - Cynthia Rothrock and Hilda
Wilson

Grandmaster Wilson at Bruce and Brandon Lee resting place

Notes

剛軟拳法白龍道

白蓮拳法

Notes

剛軟拳法白龍道

白蓮拳法

剛軟拳法白龍道白蓮拳法

Notes

_____

_____

_____

_____

_____

_____

_____

_____

_____

_____

_____

_____

_____

_____

_____

_____

_____

_____

_____

_____

_____

_____

_____

_____

Notes

剛軟拳法白龍道

白蓮拳法

CPSIA information can be obtained at www.ICGtesting.com
Printed in the USA
BVOW07s1837150414

350739BV00005B/84/P